71 Solutions

for Peace, Prosperity, and Harmony with Our Planet

Scott Allen Bunn

ISBN: 978-1-716-31712-5
Copyright 2020
Imprint: Lulu.com

Acknowledgments

This book would not have been possible without the guiding light, the love, and the mentoring of so many people.

I would first like to thank my parents, Tom and Cindy, for being loving providers for my and my brother's livelihoods. They worked hard to make sure we had everything we needed while teaching us practical life skills, and instilling one heck of a work ethic. They helped us get through college and, at the same time, quit their jobs to start a family construction company near Clemson, SC where my brother Matt and I were going to school. This provided us with jobs while we were in school and helped to create a foundation for my career. I would also like to thank my big brother Matt for taking care of me when things got rough, for encouraging me to take that leaping next step when I needed it, and for helping me keep the focus and dedication that I needed to succeed.

The mentors, teachers, authors and speakers both near and far have been an amazing guiding force, helping me climb the ladder of life in a way that serves. Some of you know who you are, and some of you may never know just how much of a positive impact you have had on my life. Thank you Neal Workman, Robert Krieger, Nat Bradford, Tradd Cotter, David Thornton, Tai Lopez, Dan Lier, Naveed Bhatti, Cheryl Lecroy, Sara Hoff, Meredith & Tucker Garrigan, Tony Robbins, Derek Holzhausen, Josh Risley, John C. Maxwell, Brené Brown, Michael Beckwith, Geoff Lawton, Joel Salatin, Angela Duckworth, and so many more for guiding me, and for being a service to humanity.

A huge thanks the contributors of this book. Without Andy Lemons and Paula Appling, this book would still be a messy voice text in my smartphone's notepad. Andy has dedicated what seems like a decent fraction of his life to getting this book out of my head and refined into this context that you are now holding in your hands. He essentially took my mumbo jumbo and made it into Louisiana Gumbo. Paula then joined the team in the final year of production to fine tune, perfect, and publish. Randall Davis, Alexandra Fleit, and David Coombs inspired the forward, quotes, and questions. Thank you all so much for helping me complete this work.

And finally, to my wife Chelsea; Thank you for your love, support, friendship and guidance. And thank you for crafting the beautiful watercolor icons representing the 7 levels in this book.

Table of Contents

Foreword

Scott Bunn's *71 Solutions* is a timely, accessible guide to the practical choices available to all of us that will make the world a better place. The huge scale of the challenges we face today, from the COVID-19 pandemic to anthropogenic climate change, can make it feel as though our problems are too big for anything we could individually do to have any effect. In a compact, readable form, *71 Solutions* describes concrete steps we can take to channel that hopelessness into acts that bring us closer to living in a sustainable way.

David Coombs
November 2020

Introduction

It is hard work to be conscious all the time of the consequences of our actions, so interconnected are we to the world and to each other.

This book is a guide for anyone who wants to take small steps to live with a lower carbon footprint while increasing financial stability and quality of life. This is a goal we can all attain, indeed must attain if we are to continue to inhabit Earth. As the ancient proverb holds, every journey begins with a single step. This guide offers 71 of them. Although short enough to read in a few hours, the solutions in this book will take time to implement.

A revolution is upon us. Sudden, rapid changes in the climate, the economy, and our social construct are forcing us to make radical adjustments. Fear not and see the opportunity to rethink our relationship to the rest of the world. If we face the coming challenges with honest and open hearts and minds, we will have no choice but to finally stop seeing ourselves as masters of nature and to start realizing that we are part of an interdependent whole. Everything is interconnected. The sooner we realize this, the sooner we can start living intentionally while securing a safe and healthy future for all living things.

This does not mean we should go off the grid or abandon the economy. The word "economy" originally meant "the care of our home," and it can mean this again. We do not seek for the goal of individual self-sufficiency, but rather collective sustainability in our shared home. Perhaps the most pressing question we face as a species is: how can we create a healthy, equitable economy without compromising the environment? We are beginning to see solutions to this problem arise all around, from the grass roots to the corporate sector; from small community gardens, workshops and community potlucks to benefit corporations and other similar businesses that are mission-based alternatives to exploitative industries.

But we do not have to wait for businesses to change. We can each act now, in our cities, in our neighborhoods, and especially in our own homes, apartments, and backyards. The solutions in this book are designed to solve challenges we all face, together and individually, in the push for a sustainable future. Some solutions originally pertained to specific problems, but can be applied more widely, for example, see the Permaculture Principles from David Holmgren and Bill Mollison in Chapters 33 and 61. Some of these solutions may seem out of reach, or may not be applicable to you at this time. However, the principles in this book are timeless and can be revisited as needed. These solutions are developed in such a way that they are easy, convenient and inexpensive. In short, they are *doable*, so they will stick. It's all about changing our daily habits and ways of thinking.

The problems that we face as a species may seem immense and hopelessly complicated. I believe the root of the solutions remain simple, and should be made accessible to everyone.

Human induced climate change, disease, war, resource depletion, terrorism, inequality, and, as I finish writing this book, a global pandemic, are only some of the major obstacles that stand between us and a better world. It is natural to feel overwhelmed by all of it. Some are even tempted to see our times as the end times, an "apocalypse." At its origin, from Greek *apokaluptein*, the word "apocalypse" simply means "to uncover or reveal." The world is in constant change, as it always has been and must ever be. Now may be the end of the world as we know it, but this may be true of every single moment of our lives, as they pass on to reveal a new world. This book is about grasping the infinite potential of the present moment to enact change for the better.

People often think that sustainable living means that you have to be totally self-sufficient: growing all of your own food on your own land, making your own clothing and tools, providing for yourself and your family without any help. This is not true, and certainly not a goal that most of us hope to achieve. Think about it like this: Humans have been able to live on planet Earth since the beginning without "outside help." We have never actually needed resources from beyond this planet to survive. A person or a community can provide for one's self while destroying an ecosystem, but this often takes multiple generations, and therefore is difficult for any one person to see. If we cannot sustain a way of life indefinitely without causing extinction, unnecessary suffering, or making life impossible for future generations, then *we are not sustainable*. We all must make the changes, so that we all, now and to come, can sustain not only ourselves, but future generations, in addition to non human species. Also consider this: if you are part of the whole and the whole is not sustainable, then neither are you. In other words, we all need to achieve this together, so lets get on with it.

All 71 solutions are organized into 7 levels. If we want to do this, we must address all 7 levels. Some, and in fact most, solutions apply to more than one level. Those 7 levels are:

1. Sustenance - food and water
2. Shelter - the clothing, homes, and buildings in which we reside
3. Community - our friends, family people in which we share our lives
4. Environment - everything and everyone else outside of your community
5. Economy - the monetary world and means of exchange
6. Energy - electricity, fuel, and transportation
7. Government - natural and non-natural systems that influence the playing field.

I would like to invite you to visit 71Solutions.org for additional resources, and to share your journey on our forum.

About the Author

Born in Findlay, Ohio, a city of industrial farming and manufacturing, I grew up tending to horses on a small farm and spent a lot of time working with my dad, who was always building something. When I was 11, my family moved to Charleston, SC where I finished grade school, and for the first time, experienced cultural diversity. I attended Clemson University for a degree in Business Management while working part time with my family's construction company. We would build and sell custom homes as our primary business operation. During my senior year at Clemson, I built a home with some friends, with an intention to sell it after a few years. A few years later in 2008, the economy crashed and my journey towards sustainability began.

Businesses were closing, people were losing their homes, and I had a brand new car, college loans, and a mortgage. Thanks to a diversity of skill sets and some of the solutions that I have listed in this book, I was able to stay afloat. Meanwhile, I spent the next year and a half researching why the economy crashed, learned a lot about how the world works, and frankly, became quite frustrated.

I ended up turning my home into an intentional community with the goal to transition from standard to sustainable. With a small group of founding visionaries, we named it the Seneca Treehouse Project (STP). In case you're wondering how we came up with the name, we have a tree house in the backyard, and we are located in Seneca, SC. Since the beginning of STP, I have had the opportunity to work, learn, and live with many wonderful people. They all bring their own stories, knowledge, and experiences to the community and we all share a sense of a responsible use of resources, learning to live with nature rather than to control it, and contributing to a healthy economy.

The Seneca Treehouse is our home base, and the backbone for our parent company. Treehouse Internatural, Inc. consists of STP, Treehouse Trade School, and Amity Builders. Our mission and vision is to help each other design, build, and live in harmony with our planet so that we can all live in prosperity today without compromising the generations of tomorrow. Treehouse has a two-part goal:

1. To develop a trade school for all ages focused on leadership training for sustainability. We want to help people start businesses that are

good for people and the planet. The majority of the proceeds from this book will go to the development of Treehouse Trade School.

2. While offering apprenticeship opportunities for Tree Scouts, we will continue to develop permaculture learning centers and demonstrations sites around the globe while working with local communities and municipalities.

Thank you for buying this book and for taking action to be a part of the solution.

1 Value Yourself

You are a slice of perfection

The first step is the foundation for the rest of the journey. The fact that you are reading this book means that you have already set in pursuit of positive change in yourself, your home, and the world. On this path you will face many obstacles, distractions and pitfalls. It may seem easier at times to go back to the status quo. How can you stay focused and empowered in your purpose? I believe it starts with valuing yourself.

Make a list of the answers to these questions and use these answers as a guide in moving forward through the rest of the book. I promise the whole book is not going to be a lot of list making, just a few of the first steps.

1. What are some of the things you enjoy doing most?
2. What gets you really excited?
3. What is on your bucket list?
4. What are some of your strongest traits and talents?
5. What skills have you acquired through training and practice?
6. Do you prefer spending time with people, or spending time alone?
7. Who are some of your heroes and why?
8. If you could have a career helping people or the planet, do you know what it might be?
9. What else is just awesome about you? Don't be shy.

Now, write a personal mission statement. Use the answers to these questions to help you come up with that statement. Try to keep it short, roughly 7-12 words. My personal mission is: *Help each other live in harmony with our planet.* As simple as it may seem, It took me several years to refine that, so don't be discouraged if you can't nail it down right away.

ACTION IDEAS

Use the space below to answer the questions from the previous page.

Value Yourself

2 Value Your Neighbor

"There is no impact without contact." ~Andrew Fraley, STP resident

When I first began my journey towards sustainability, I told a friend that I would have to travel around the world to meet like-minded people. "No, you don't," she said. "Just meet your neighbors." She was right. Wonderful and talented people are all around us, we just have to go out and meet them. We live right next to an RV campground that can get a little rowdy. At first glance, I didn't think anyone from the campground would be interested in what we were doing. After giving tours, and sharing our story with our friends in the campground, they began to open up too, and before I knew it, they started getting involved. Some of the older kids began giving tours to the younger kids. One of the teenagers did an internship with us, and to this day the relationships continue to unfold. I believe the secret is common ground with a heavy dose of humility. We all share the same needs and desires, yet our passions and resources vary. This means we can all help each other. Interdependence, it turns out, is stronger than independence.

Here are some ideas and events you can hold to strengthen your community:

1. Host a monthly open house and potluck. This is a great time to meet new friends, catch up with the old, and share current events. This can be done at a church or a park if someone's home does not suit.
2. My neighbors do an annual cookout and holiday karaoke, which I think is pretty cool.
3. Adopt a neighborhood Trash Cleanup.
4. A community board, where everyone can communicate, leave lost and found items, and post events.

As far as reaching out to new people, you could go door to door. If you decide to do that, for safety, go as a group, and perhaps offer them something tasty, like some extra produce, or a baked good. Digitally, you could start a Facebook group for the community, a Meetup, or whatever new digital doohickey you have access to.

Once you get together — and this is the hard part, but the best part — try to really engage in meaningful conversation. Try to really get to know someone rather than just making small talk about the weather. Ask them questions about themselves. People love to talk about themselves.

Some ideas for questions:

- What are you into? What do you like to do?
- What do you do for work? How did you get into that?
- Do you have family close by?
- What do you like about this neighborhood? What don't you like?

If you are an organizer, you could keep track of this information for future community development projects.

ACTION IDEAS

What is one way of getting to know my neighbors that I can commit to doing this week?

Value Your Neighbor

3 Set the Principles

"Policies are many, Principles are few, Policies will change, Principles never do."
~ John C. Maxwell, Author

A principle is a simple truth that serves as a foundation for a system or behavior. It is a basic law, a function, a rule, or a standard. Throughout this book, I highlight the permaculture principles. Finding and setting principles at the beginning serves as a guide to help you reach your goal. The principles outlined here will be elaborated in the following chapters. You may want to adopt other principles, or set some of your own. They could be deep meaningful principles like "all life is to be treated with compassion" or something perhaps on the other end of the spectrum like "starch is for thickening." Take some time to think about some key principles that you want to use as a guide for moving forward.

Here are some ideas to consider.

- Think before you buy
- Be kind to all living things
- Plant food and let food grow
- Feed myself so that I can have the strength to feed others
- Listen first, talk later
- Teach others to fish
- Help only where help is desired

moving more keeps the body moving

ACTION IDEAS

Use the space below to jot down your principles.

Set the Principles

4 Identify Assets and Minimize Liabilities

"Rich people acquire assets. The poor and middle class acquire liabilities that they think are assets. - Robert Kiyosaki, Businessman and Author

This step is not an action item. It is a precursor for the following steps to help you identify things that are feeding you versus things that are feeding on you.

An asset is an item of value owned. Typically, assets can be easily converted into cash. Assets can be tangible, like land and equipment, or intangible, like a patent or copyright. A liability is anything you are liable for or owe money to. So if you purchase a house with a loan, the house itself is an asset, and the mortgage is a liability. The difference in the value of the house and the money owed is equity.

Some assets depreciate, like tools, equipment, structures and vehicles. Something that I have come to see as a builder and permaculturist is that as soon as I finish building something, it begins to depreciate. As soon as I buy a piece of equipment, it begins losing value. On the flip side, when I turn a yard into a garden, or plant a tree, it will continue to grow and develop on its own, appreciating in value for the life of the tree, meanwhile producing new trees, food, medicine, and beauty along the way.

It is important to make the most of assets during their life, to minimize depreciating assets, and to invest in things that are likely to produce. Invest in assets that are sure to hold or grow in value like knowledge, quality land, secure stocks, and the often overlooked edible and medicinal plants.

Assets can turn into cash with passive income, active income, or by selling. Active income requires your labor. A hammer, for example, would usually be an active income asset unless you were to rent it out or have an employee that uses it. An apartment could produce more passive income. When you take inventory in the next step, under the income column, put an "A" for active, "P" for passive, or an "S" to mark for sale. This will give you an idea about how to best utilize what you have to gain the most ground.

ACTION IDEAS

What are your assets?

What are your liabilities?

Identify Assets and Minimize Liabilities

5 Organize

Once organized, life becomes easier. This solution, like many others, can be applied anywhere in life from your physical space and belongings, to your routine and way of thinking. For me, if things are not organized, I feel stressed, but it's not always an obvious stress. It's like a background stressor. If there is physical clutter, there will be mental clutter and vice versa.

Think about all the time you've spent looking for something that you either misplaced, or it just didn't have a home to begin with. If you add up all of that time, just think about how much more life you would have to do other things. I have collectively spent at least a few months of my life looking for things, and having to buy new tools because of a lack of organization. That time, and money might have paid for a vacation of a lifetime.

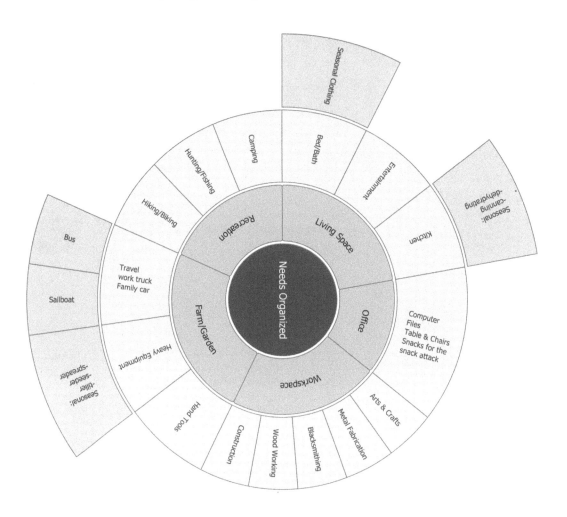

Organizing can be a tricky task, so you may have to find a friend who can help. If you know someone who is obsessive, this could be a bonus. If you have a lot of stuff, mind maps can be helpful for organizing thoughts, by grouping like elements while considering frequency of use. This is my mind map (next page): the categories are in yellow, the items often used are blue, and seasonal items are green. I try to keep certain categories close together if the items are interchangeable or related.

After getting things organized, if you are a natural mess maker like me, it might help to create a routine maintenance plan or at least a monthly reminder on your calendar to check yourself. Also note that even if you are not a mess maker, it will still unravel, because entropy _lack of order_ is constantly at work on integrity. After establishing a sense of order, it becomes much easier to do the following chapters in the book, but before you go ahead and read through the next chapters, so you can see the bigger picture.

ACTION IDEAS

Organize

6 Take Inventory

You are on a life changing journey. It is important to know what you own, and exactly where it is located so that you can maximize its potential. It is key to not just organize what you have, but to take inventory. Your inventory is the total stock of anything you own. This list will be used throughout the book, and you will want to add or subtract from it later. For now, just list the item, location and a brief description. Create a chart and leave enough room to add columns for later. If it's trash, refer to **The 5 R's** before throwing it into the garbage. The following are the kinds of things to look for.

1. Tools: hand tools, power tools, tractor, welder, sewing machine, paint brushes, etc.

2. Transportation: cars, boats, airplanes, bicycles, spaceships, etc.

3. Real Estate: land and buildings

4. Intellectual property: patents, copyrights, trademarks etc.

5. Electronics: Books, computers, cell phones, drones, web sites

6. Recreational equipment: exercising, hunting, fishing, boating, climbing, camping

7. Kitchen Supplies: Appliances, expensive glassware, cutlery

8. Furniture

9. Clothing

This is part of your foundation. Refer to these two lists throughout the rest of the book, and update it as needed.

Item	Location	Description	Asset	Liability	Should I keep it?	Value	
chainsaw	shop	tool	x		yes	$300.00	<-- Example
jet ski	garage	toy		x	sell it	$3,000.00	<-- Example

ACTION IDEAS

As you take inventory, you will likely discover you have more than you need. What could you do with the excess that might benefit your community?

Take Inventory

7 Assess Needs and Wants

Every item impacts the environment

Now that you know what you own and where it is. Take the list that you made in **Take Inventory** and add a "need" column. Label each item 1, 2, or 3 according to the following rule.

1. Do I need this to survive? This includes sustenance, shelter, and primary tools.

2. Does this make life more efficient and convenient?

3. Is this cool, a trinket, nice to have, or excess baggage?

You really shouldn't have too many #1 items. If you finish the list and don't have anything in the #3 category, try again. If you are unsure of whether or not you actually need it, ask yourself, "what would I do if I didn't have it?" Take a smart phone for example: As a business owner I need to be in contact with people, stay up on current events, and share progress with people. However, I do not need it to survive. If I did not have a smartphone and I wanted to maintain the quality of our company, I would need a landline/regular cell, a camera, a computer, a GPS, and several subscriptions to magazines and newspapers, plus various other tools to do what many apps are capable of. Here, even though a smartphone is a great choice to make things more economical, I do not need it to survive, so it would be classified as a #2. We are going to use this solution in the following, **Less Clutter, More Life**. Consider this with your future purchasing decisions and remember the opening phrase, "every item impacts the environment."

ACTION IDEAS

Assess Needs and Wants

8 Less Clutter, More Life

"The first step in crafting the life you want is to get rid of everything you don't."
~Joshua Becker, Author

Now that you have a list of all of your stuff and the importance of each item, let's take it one step further. With this solution, we are going to reduce the **quantity** of things in your life, and add to the **quality** of life. Clearing your space of clutter will free your mind and your physical space. Fewer distractions increase the capability to be and do what you want. Simply stated, **Life is easier without clutter.**

For now, let's look primarily at the #3 items you don't need, while considering some of the #2 items that make life more convenient.

What to do with all that stuff? Sell it. Lately, I find *Facebook Marketplace* is quite effective, however, garage sales, local markets, *eBay, Etsy,* and *Craigslist* are other decent options. Set this money aside to invest in something that will help you live more sustainably. Don't just buy more stuff. If you can't sell it, give it away. If you post a free stuff ad on craigslist, someone will probably show within the hour. If you can't give it away, see the step **The 5 R's**.

Now that you have free space in your home, you could get creative with it: you could rent it out, or sell the house and downsize, or put up some family or friends in need, etc. Give up the stuff, and get down with being whom you want to be, and make the most of life. You will have more time to live, to learn, and to do the things you love.

ACTION IDEAS

What can I get rid of?

Less Clutter, More Life

9 The 5 R's

The greatest threat to our planet is the belief that someone else will save it."
~Robert Swan, Author

Consider these R's in the following order. It's a simple concept with infinite possibilities. Share your creativity with us at 71Solutions.org.

Reduce - Reduce what you buy to begin with. Everything you buy costs you time and money. Also consider the things that you don't buy but get anyway, like straws, styrofoam cups, and ketchup packets.

Reuse - For what you do buy, choose things that can be reused, or try to reuse what you already have. Start with things like stainless steel water bottles, food carryout containers, grocery bags, coffee cups, etc.

Repair - In today's fast paced society, it's so easy to throw things away when they quit working. Purchase high quality equipment that lasts a long time and is repairable. Cheaper items actually cost more to repair than to replace. There are many great general part companies out there like eReplacementparts.com and toolpartsdirect.com, and you can usually find specific brand replacement parts too. If you can't find replacement parts or the item is too far gone, refer to the next item on this list.

Repurpose - This is where creativity comes in. My friend Kevin is an artist who makes "Art Outta Parts" and he makes some sweet practical art. Learning how to weld or forge metal can be extremely helpful in the journey towards sustainability, but there are infinite ways to repurpose things besides crafty decor.

Recycle - The last resort before the landfill. At all costs, try to keep items out of the landfill. If your local municipality does not recycle, you may have to go the extra effort to travel to the next town. In our county, the standard items like glass, plastic, steel and aluminum, are recycled, but wax cartons, styrofoam, or plastic wrappers are not. Search around and see if you can find a center for hard to recycled materials.

ACTION IDEAS

Name one of each R that you can commit to this week.

Reduce -

Reuse -

Repair -

Repurpose -

Recycle -

The 5 R's

10 Tool Sharing

*"A tool is but the extension of a man's hand, and a machine is
but a complex tool. And he that invents a machine augments the power
of a man and the well-being of mankind."*
~Henry Ward Beecher

I have over 700 tools. I am a builder, so I use a lot of these tools; however I seldom have a job that requires me to use more than 15-20 of these tools at one time. Think of how many people own a lawnmower, and how often each person uses that lawnmower. In the grand scheme of things, it is quite wasteful for everyone to own their own tools, especially if they don't use them on a regular basis. Tools rust, rot, and depreciate even when they are not being used, especially if they have moving parts.

This solution is about creating a tool library, tool co-op, or other tool-sharing program. Tools require maintenance and have a cost associated with use, so here are a few ways to set it up.

- Stand alone library, similar to a book library where tools are free to use and there is an annual fee and volunteer labor to cover maintenance and real estate. This works well for garden and hand tools where the cost to use is low.

- Equipment rental centralized location - users pay a fee to use the tools per hour. This is better for mechanical tools and equipment where cost of use is higher.

- Decentralized locations such as several individuals' homes or workshops.

The following is in no way legal advice, but some things you may want to consider when setting up the operation.

- Agreements to protect all users and clearly define use
- Standard operating procedures for proper use, systems check protocol, maintenance, and repair schedules for each tool
- Liability waiver for all users
- Ensure each user is insured in case they do have an accident

Some tool libraries and maker spaces require each user to be certified on each tool. Usually, to get certified, the user must demonstrate proper use of those tools.

We use a Google spreadsheet to list all tools, and you could easily add maintenance schedules, replacement costs, and desired rental rates. Most tools have a general life expectancy. They need to be maintained, rebuilt, and replaced. Tools also cost money to store. Whether it's an air-conditioned shop space, storage container, or just a raw piece of land, a cost is always associated with storage.

Many great resources are available for tool sharing programs. Check out https://sharestarter.org/tools/ for a great start with sample documents, business plan, and other methods to get you started.

ACTION IDEAS

What tools do you have to share? What tools do you need?

11 List Your Expenses

"Beware of little expenses; a small leak will sink a great ship." ~Benjamin Franklin

In 2008, I was fresh out of college with a quarter million-dollar mortgage, new truck payments, and a grocery bill of nearly $800/month. When the economy crumbled in late 2008, my journey to sustainability began. I had to figure out what I could do without and what I could provide for myself. The first step was to make a list of all yearly, monthly, and weekly expenses. This is a good way to see not only where you are spending your money, but also where your time and attention are being focused. Try it. And be accurate; you can look back on your bank statements to find exact figures. Don't forget about those long-term expenses, and the expenses that are irregular, like getting your propane tank filled or paying for your website subscription once every 3 years. Also, remember to factor in wear and tear (that is, routine repairs) on, for instance, your car or home. The following may be some of your expenses.

- Housing (rent or mortgage)
- Car Payments
- Travel expenses - roughly $.65/mile wear and tear
- Groceries
- Libations
- Utilities
- Monthly subscriptions
- Savings
- Investing
- Health insurance
- Donations
- Credit Card Payments
- Other

Now, use this list to see where your money is going, and how you can eliminate or redirect some expenses. My first step after listing my expenses was to turn my mortgage expense into rental income by renting out my house, which later allowed me to transform the property into something better. Then it became time to grow some groceries!

ACTION IDEAS

What are your greatest expenses? Where can you cut back?

List Your Expenses

12 Vote with Your Dollar

"Buy the change you want to see in the world." ~*Andy Lemons, Ph.D.*

Money… I used to hate the idea of money. Consequently, during that period of my life, I didn't have much. Quoting Timothy 6:10, "The love of money is the root of all evil." So if I hate it, I don't have it, and if I love it, does it makes me evil? I believe there is more to it than that. Money is a powerful tool. I think of it as an enabling unit, and with that enabling unit, you can choose what you do with it. Money is a powerful tool, and tools treated carelessly often become weapons. We tend to blame the irresponsible corporations for all of the destruction they cause in the pursuit of profit. For some corporations, this may be true, and it is also true that without the buyer, there would be no corporation.

The cycle often goes like this:

1. We demand low prices.
2. The producer meets that demand by any means necessary.
3. We buy cheap products.
4. We get upset when companies enslave people, or destroy an ecosystem.
5. We continue to want the lowest price and …
6. Go back to the store to buy some more!

Have you noticed the missing piece? Where and when do we re-examine our deep responsibility in this cycle?

Think of money as a unit of power. Wherever it is, it empowers. If you have it, you are empowered. If you give it to someone else, you empower them. When money leaves our hands, we think of it as money spent. We wash our hands of it.

Try instead, to think of all of your spending as an investment. Even if you are not getting money back on the investment, you are getting something in return. Whatever you invest in, you encourage. I challenge you to research the ethics and ecological practices of the companies and the kinds of products you invest in.

ACTION IDEAS

How do you think about money? How can you change your vote?

All God-given.
Not "ours" to begin with.

Vote with Your Dollar

13 Adopt the Pace of Nature

"The Biomimicry Revolution introduces an era based not on what we can extract from nature, but on what we can learn from her."
~Janine Benyus, Natural Sciences Writer

We love nature. We want it in our lives. Just think of all of the products that are made to mimic nature, like fake plants, laminate wood flooring and sound machines that lull us to sleep with sounds of ocean waves and squawking seagulls. Humans are drawn back to nature no matter how much we try to escape it. When we breathe, when we eat, when we drink, and when we urinate and defecate, we are taking from nature, becoming nature, and ultimately returning part of ourselves back to nature. And if you're uncomfortable with any talk of defecating, this is a perfect example of how disconnected from nature we really are. Eventually, each of us returns entirely back to nature.

As much as we, as individuals, love and appreciate nature, as a society we tend to try to force nature to do what we want, when we want it. We often destroy it and a part of ourselves in the process. When we slow down and reflect on our own cycles of moods, digestion, sickness and strength, we see there is no taking the human out of nature's pace or nature's pace out of the human. The harder we try, the more diseased we become. We **are** internatural.

There are many things we can do to adopt nature's pace, to build upon the internatural. It is not just about "slowing down," though scheduling a meditation or mindfulness practice every day can help us find pause and rest to reflect on our real, natural tempo.

Start by asking the question "what would nature do?," or "what would our ancestors have done before modern technology?"

ACTION IDEAS

What are some ways that you can "adopt nature's pace" in your own life?

Adopt the Pace of Nature

14 Focus on the Light

"Imagination is everything. It is the preview of life's coming attractions."
~Albert Einstein

What you think about, you bring about. Every thought is like a tiny prayer, or a vote for what you want. Sometimes we get what we want, and sometimes we get things that we do not. Perhaps not everything that happens in our lives is a result of our thoughts, and perhaps it is. Focus on solutions, gratitude, and what you want to bring about in your life, or for others.

When I first heard of the law of attraction, i.e., "What you think about you bring about," I didn't know if it would work, so I just went all in and tried it. At the time, I had a small amount of work in my job folder, and a huge debt to pay. I said to myself, I would like $300,000 worth of work. I didn't just say it, I felt it. I meditated on it. I prayed and asked for it. While doing no additional advertising, within a day I started receiving calls. Within two weeks, I had $169,000 worth of jobs estimated. Prior to that, I never had more than a few thousand dollars in my job folder at one time. At that point, I got overwhelmed and decided that I needed to stop estimating jobs and focus on the work. The phone quit ringing and I began focusing on earning the income that I needed. At that point in my life, I realized that thoughts **do** affect reality.

The words that we speak or think influence ourselves, other life forms, and perhaps even more. When I tell people this, they agree with me when thinking about how it affects themselves, but sometimes find it ridiculous that our thoughts can affect reality outside of our own bodies. One thing is for certain, you will never know until you try it. Try to focus on one thing with certainty for a while, and see if your world starts to turn. If you don't believe it will work, then you are probably right. If you do believe it, then you are also probably right because it all starts with your system of beliefs.

Be conscious of all of your thoughts. Studies have shown that we have conscious and subconscious thoughts, for some people up to 600 words a minute. Try to be conscious of your thoughts and steer them towards the life you want.

34

Sometimes we are dealt a poor hand. The key, then, is what you tell yourself and others about the situation you are in. For instance, if you end up with cancer, some people might say "I have cancer," while you could say instead, "I am overcoming cancer" or "My body has an amazing ability to heal." One thing I find helpful in manifesting positive thinking is to make a dream board. If you are unfamiliar with this idea, a dream board is just a poster board or could be simply a background on your computer or phone to post pictures, words, and other visuals that you wish to manifest. We all use the law of attraction whether we know it or not. Try to hone in on your thoughts habits. How are they affecting your life? What can you do to change them?

ACTION IDEAS

What are some thoughts you currently have about yourself that could be holding you back right now?

Focus on the Light

What new thoughts do you want to instill?

15 Compost

"When a flower doesn't bloom, you fix the environment in which it grows, not the flower." - Alexander Den Heijer, Inspirational Speaker

In the United States alone, according to the USDA, food waste is approximately 30-40% of the entire food supply. That's about 133 BILLION pounds of food amounting to $161 billion dollars annually.

Typically, food waste that ends up in a landfill is buried and becomes anaerobic producing methane, a prominent greenhouse gas.

If instead we compost our food waste, either through commercial or independent composting systems, those nutrients become available to soil building organisms which **is** the major contributing factor to soil health. Healthy soil grows healthy plants which grow healthy people. It is crucial to keep those nutrients in the life cycle.

Healthy soil also provides greater water retention. That means less flash flooding and more water to evaporate into the air, which leads to more cloud cover as well as climate stability. (see also *5s's of Water* & *Build Healthy Soil*)

A friend worked with the bio-systems engineering department at Clemson University to create a commercial scale recycling facility utilizing food scraps from 7 dining facilities, 3 sports stadiums, and special events. This is just one facility in one town. Imagine the effect this would have on a larger scale. No more "wasted food," and no more mining for fossil fuel derived fertilizer.

At the Seneca Treehouse, we have multiple methods for composting, including black soldier flies, feeding food scraps directly to chickens and using manure, vermiculture (worms), or a simple compost bin. If you don't have money to buy the above mentioned, try this method: Put the food scraps in a 3-5 gallon black pot. Once the pot is full, flip it over in your garden in its final destination.

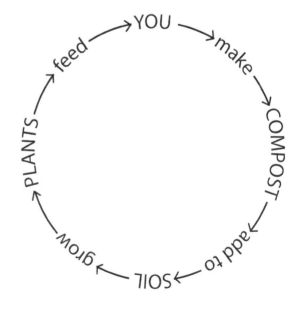

From there it breaks down, still inside the pot where it is protected from chickens, but accessible to insects. After a few months, pick up the pot, and spread out the newly composted food waste right where it sits. Then repeat this process in a new location.

ACTION IDEAS

Do you already compost? If not, how can you get started?

All food scraps? = what about racoons + opossum?

Compost

37

16 Be Politically Involved

"If you want to change the politician, redirect the wind." ~anonymous

What if we had a political system that could account for all parties and decide with a centralized system? I call it the political flower. The petals are the parties, and the center is the non-biased, incorruptible, science-based, decision making system. I know this is a pie in the sky idea, so for now, please vote, and consider the following when voting.

Voting for those who will represent you in national and local politics is an essential first step in citizenship, but to really make a difference in our community, we have to step up our level of involvement. It's important to know the different levels of government and the key responsibilities of each. Figure out who is running for each level and vote. Vote for someone inspiring who will be a good leader while bringing people together. I believe, it is crucial to have a leader whose words and actions unite us. A divided nation will fall. Learn what people stand for. Don't vote for someone just because they are a Democrat or Republican, or because of their race or gender. Research the history of the candidate's public work, and pay close attention to their track record.

	Legislative (create the law)	Executive (enforce the law)	Judicial (judge the law)
Federal	Congress House of Representatives Senate	President Vice President Cabinet	US Supreme Court US Court of Appeals Military Tribunals
State	State House of Representatives State Senate	Governor State Police	State Supreme Court State Court of Appeals
Local	County Council City Council School Boards	Mayor City & County Police Chief	County and City Court Family Court

Another way to get involved is to attend town hall meetings. Most towns have monthly meetings discussing a variety of issues, events and developments. Usually, the public is welcome to join. It's not something you need to do every month, but it is good to do a few times a year, if for nothing else, just to gain experience.

You can also address your legislators directly and urge them to protect people and our planet. Take small steps and be specific. Enroll others to take action too.

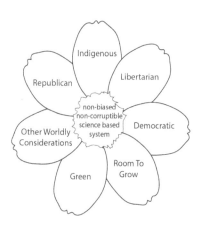

And if you really want to dive in, you could become the elected official. Direct action, no less than voting, is a part of your freedom and power as an American citizen. As it seems, to get elected is a combination of popularity and advertising. If you do this, please remain authentic and incorruptible.

ACTION IDEAS

What are some personal steps you can take to become a more informed and civic-minded voter?

17 Read the Label

Labels on food products are sometimes helpful, and sometimes misleading. The front face, with the cartoon characters, the homey imagery, and the short phrases like "natural" and "green" is the least helpful part of the label, but not the only misleading part. What matters more is the ingredients list under all the often deceptive numbers and percentages. A product's ingredients are listed in decreasing order. Some libraries have a special food dictionary just for food additives. You would need to be a biochemist to understand them all. As a consumer, what I want to learn from a label includes: where the food was farmed, where it was packaged, where it was shipped from, how many ingredients were added in processing, its expiration date, and its nutritional value.

Look for high-quality, nutritional food. Look for simple ingredients and whole foods. As a general rule, eat foods with 6 ingredients or fewer and that you can pronounce all of the ingredients. And remember, just because a food is distributed locally does not mean it is grown locally. And unless it is a dried grain, dehydrated, or frozen, it *should* probably expire within a few weeks of purchase. If not, it may be considered a "dead" food, which is basically like eating sugar coated cardboard.

ACTION IDEAS

Read the Label

18 Seasonal Connection

"Embrace the seasons and cycles in your life. There is magic in change."
~Bronnie Ware, Author

Consider that part of living in a place is to live within its climate. Most people are used to buying the same foods year round from a grocery store and living in air-conditioned homes. Did you know that your store-bought food travels an average of 1200 miles before reaching your plate? Eating strawberries from Chile in December is to be disconnected from the seasons, and the real world cost is greater than what you pay out at the checkout.

Rather than changing your environment to suit your needs, rethink your needs to suit the environment. Learn which foods are grown in your community and when. Eat food from your local farmer, and you will truly avail yourself of what is in season. It can also add more excitement to the dinner table.

Consider the seasons when deciding what to wear inside your home. In the winter, layer up, add blankets to your bed, and find a sweet pair of slippers. Then adjust your thermostat to 60-65 degrees. I dare you to go lower! In the summer, use fans, blinds and natural circulation. Adjust your thermostat to 75-80 (the EPA recommends 78) degrees. This will save on heating and cooling costs.

ACTION IDEAS

How might you change your life to be more in pace with the seasons?

Seasonal Connection

19 Open Source

We tend to be possessive of ideas we think of as our own. We are led to believe that ideas are capital to be hoarded. But can ideas really belong to individuals? What if two or more people have the same idea? What if an idea is just a possibility that was always there, hiding in plain sight all along, just waiting for someone to look at it in the right way?

What if you shared the idea with the world, and co-developed it with others? Doing this would allow the people around you to excel, creating stronger and more active communities.

I spent a few weeks working with Marcin Jakubowski at Open Source Ecology in Missouri. I helped build the trencher, one of the 50 machines in their Global Village Construction Set. The process they have for creating something open source is detailed and effective. Design and building are group efforts and the result is a form of appropriate technology. That is, the idea whose method, materials, and design can be relatively easily accessed globally. For more information about the Global Village Construction Set, go to https://www.opensourceecology.org/.

Which do you think would be better: to discover an idea and hold on to it with the possibility that it could be produced one day, or to share that idea with the community so that anyone can use it? If you are leaning towards the former, go for it and get it out there already! Otherwise, consider trying to make it open source.

ACTION IDEAS

What are some open source technologies that have changed the world for the better? Do you have any ideas that you would like to share?

Open Source

20 Stop the Bleeding

"Happiness comes from making good choices.
Integrity, energy, perseverance, and courage all contribute." ~Mary Pipher, Author

This is a principle step to assess the energy leaks in our lives. Think of your whole existence as a living thing. Step back and see your life for what it is: your home, job, family, friends, and hobbies all affect the overall health of your existence. This step is about improving efficiency by first identifying where your life energy is dissipating. This section is about people and career. Another area of concern focuses on finances (see **List Your Expenses** and **Purge Unnecessary Expenses & Invest**).

Every moment counts. Is your time invested producing a return, or adding value to your life, or is it being lost in the gaps, cracks, and leaks? Like a wound, stopping the bleeding can sometimes be as simple as putting on a band aid and letting it heal, or it can be extremely painful like cauterizing a wound.

One of my greatest leaks used to be my interaction with people. Note that it wasn't necessarily the other person, rather how I was thinking about the other person. In part, I used to offer a lot of unsolicited advice. That was like trying to pour energy into a cup with a lid on it, only for it to be spilled off and lost in the abyss. It took me a while to realize what I was doing. I am still inclined to offer insight to a blind spot, but I am working on better strategies to save my own energy, while better contributing to others.

And then there are toxic people that you may just need to stop hanging around, no matter how much you love them. It may be easy to stop the bleeding if it's a material item that is draining you, but when working with people, the idea of "breaking up" a relationship can be difficult.

Another wounded area in my life was my job. As a builder who cares a lot about sustainable development, I kept finding myself doing jobs that were not fulfilling to my soul. After talking with a friend, I decided to focus the mission of my construction company directly towards sustainable design and development. Making this change in my career was challenging, but I decided it was better to power through the change than to go through life hating work.

ACTION IDEAS

What are some areas of your life where you might be experiencing "energy leaks?" What can you do to stop the bleeding?

Stop the Bleeding

21 Stop the Leaks in Your Home

Leak /lēk/ noun - A hole through which valuable contents accidentally pass

The average American house has enough cracks to be equivalent to having one window open all the time. Many houses are lacking in insulation in the walls and ceilings too. These issues lead to a loss of comfort and extra energy to heat and cool the structure.

Cracks can be found around windows, baseboards, attic passageways, even around outlets and switches. These may be the most obvious leaks you can patch up. Stopping such leaks is a good, concrete first in the practice of improving the integrity of a home.

For small gaps, I use caulk. For larger gaps, usually expanding foam or stuff in some fiberglass insulation. What I dislike is the fact that caulk containers are hard to recycle, but at least the metal cans from foam insulation are. Please note this may only be a net benefit in areas with extreme winters and summers. If you want to go natural, you could use cobb, which is a mixture of sand, clay, and straw. Replacing windows in an old home can also be a great investment, and it will pay you back in the form of lower power bills. Use weather stripping to seal the gaps under doors and close HVAC vents in rooms you don't use.

Another leak in your home efficiency is often the electrical leaks with appliances and electronics. There are many residual leaks when things remain plugged in and idle. You can achieve micro savings by using a splitter and turning off the splitter for all devices when not in use. Sealing up these leaks is a small and slow solution to achieve savings over the long run. You may hardly notice it, but at least you can feel confident that your home is not sinking in the sea of inefficiency.

As we seal up the cracks in our homes, radon build up can become hazardous to your health. Radon is a natural odorless gas emitted from soil and rocks due to decaying uranium. If your house is built on a slab or vent-less crawl space, odds are more likely that you may have a radon issue. You can buy a radon test kit to see if you do. Radon mitigation strategies include installation of passive or active radon exhaust systems, but this is easier to accomplish during the construction of the home. Or, installing a fresh air exchange system in the home can be a good way to control the air intake and air quality without losing valuable energy.

ACTION IDEAS

What is one recommendation you can commit to implementing in your home this week?

Stop the Leaks in Your Home

22 Energy Consciousness

Earth provides enough to satisfy every man's needs, but not every man's greed.
- Mahatma Gandhi

Are you mindful of how you use energy at home? Have you had a home energy audit? Many energy companies will come to your home and do one for free! How about energy use in public? Do you ever think about the lights in the public restrooms? On a larger scale, what sorts of energy do you depend on in your day-to-day activities, and what is the source of that energy? Where is it produced? And is it renewable or nonrenewable?

Non-renewable energy has been accumulated over the history of Earth as buried dead and decayed organic matter and other decaying elements. General examples are fossil fuels, or what some might refer to as ancient sunlight. Ancient sunlight is energy that Earth has accumulated over the millennia. Fossil fuels take millions of years to produce and we have already burnt through over half of the discovered fossil fuels on the planet in approximately 300 years. Specific examples of non-renewable energy include coal, oil, natural gas, propane, and tar sands. Non-renewables are quite dirty and dangerous when shipping, handling, and processing.

Renewable energy, or current energy, is a result of living systems. Examples include solar, wind, tidal, methane, hydroelectric, bio-diesel, geothermal, and ethanol, and wood gas. Just as its name implies, renewable energy keeps on coming. These are sources of power that are replenished continuously through living systems.

Some renewable energies are carbon neutral, meaning they pull as much carbon from the atmosphere during the production as they do when they are harvested and used. At the time of writing this, only about 10% of the world's energy consumption comes from renewable sources. The other 90%? You guessed it: non-renewable, and therefore not sustainable. One day the majority of our energy will be renewable, because in the long term, there is no other way. We don't have to wait for that day. In fact, we can't afford to. To help us get there, start by trying out some of these suggestions in your home, or at work.

The Lights: be sure to turn off the lights and the fans when you leave a room. You could install motion sensors in place of the switches for common rooms in which lights might be easily left on by accident. The motion sensors can be adjusted to turn the lights and fans off after a certain time increment. Make the switch to LED light bulbs. Don't bother with compact fluorescents.

The AC: Programmable thermostats and smart thermostats can be purchased to adjust temperatures while you are not at home, or perhaps while you are sleeping. Turning your AC off completely might result in mold and damage to your house due to high humidity, or broken water lines in the winter due to freezing temperatures. If you use electric heat, you don't want the temperature to change too rapidly; this will enable the emergency heat feature which may be more expensive than allowing the heat to increase gradually.

ACTION IDEAS

What is one practice you can commit to implementing in your home this week in order to be more energy-conscious?

Energy Consciousness

23 The Insulation Factor

Assuming you have **Stopped the Leaks in Your Home**, the majority of your heat loss in the winter may now go through the ceiling. (Yes, your January power bill is *literally* through the roof!) In the summer, the heat gain can depend a lot on your tree cover and sun exposure.

Two main categories of insulation are reflective and refractive. Reflective insulation bounces heat waves like a mirror and refractive slows the heat down, like a filter or a cushion.

Reflective insulation, or radiant barrier is a relatively inexpensive DIY insulation. It reflects thermal radiation in the same way as a thermos or a hot/cold grocery bag. It is crucial to leave an air gap when using reflective insulation, or the product will not work. Make sure you research to find a quality product.

Refractive insulation is a lightweight airy product like fiberglass, cellulose, or foam. Assuming you have an attic, ensure that you have 10 to 12 inches of fiberglass insulation above your ceiling joists. Although it can be good for wall cavities, avoid cellulose in the attic because it settles over time and eventually loses its insulation value or R-value. If you live in an older house, you may want to check the status of the walls. A thermal camera can help determine where the heat is infiltrating or escaping. You could also knock on the wall cavities to see if they sound empty.

If you are building new, consider natural building and other methods that can reduce your overall energy needs. See the chapters **Passive Heating, Passive Cooling,** and **Raise the Roof** for more information. If you are building a stick framed home, spray in foam insulation is a leader in efficiency, however there are multiple other methods for building well insulated homes such as SIPs (structurally insulated panels) and ICF (insulated concrete forms). Unfortunately, most of the foam and fiberglass insulations are considered non-biodegradable. Keep your eye out for products that do biodegrade because our homes do not last forever. There is potential for plant based biodegradable insulation, but to my knowledge, the technology has yet to hit the mainstream.

For helpful links about insulation, check out 71solutions.org.

ACTION IDEAS

Check out your attic. How thick is the insulation? What are some areas of your home where you can add reflective and/or refractive insulation?

The Insulation Factor

24a Passive Heating

Passive heating usually refers to solar heating, or using the sun's already present radiation to heat a home. Ultimately, passive heating could be accomplished by pulling heat off any existing heat source like compost, or geothermal, but in this chapter, we will focus primarily on passive solar opportunities.

A passive geothermal system can be achieved by building your home partially into the ground, but the temperature will only reach about 55 degrees depending on your region, season, and depth. To get above that, you will need to supplement, which can be achieved through passive solar heating. The proper solar orientation is key and that will vary depending on your location on the globe.

The goal is to allow direct sunlight in during the cold months and block it out during the hotter months. You can accomplish this through solar orientation of your house and building an appropriate overhang for the windows. This overhang is determined by the sun angles in the summer, in relation to the sun angles in the winter, along with the window size. Your sun angles will depend on your latitude. For help finding your sun angles, visit 71Solutions.org.

Window tinting is also important to consider. Most new windows now come with a low-e window tinting, which reduces thermal infiltration. For windows where you wish to allow solar gain, no window tinting is desired. You can also plant deciduous vines to grow over windows. The leaves will grow in the spring, shade in the summer, then drop in the fall to allow sunlight penetration through the winter. Add thermal mass such as a Trombe wall or concrete counters behind the windows to catch and store heat. The thermal mass acts like a battery, being charged during the day. Heat will emit through the night when the sun sets.

ACTION IDEAS

Are there any passive heating strategies you can implement in or around your home?

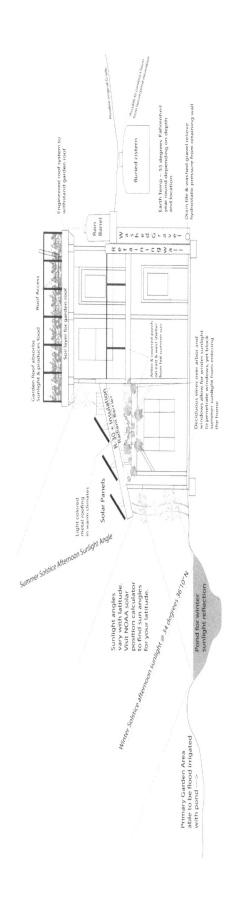

Garden Roof absorbs
Sunlight & produces food

Engineered roof system to
withstand garden roof

Roof Access

Soil layer for garden roof

Rain
Barrel

Buried cistern

Possible to construct berm
from home/pond excavation

Possible original Grade

Earth temp – 55 degrees Fahrenheit
year round depending on depth
and location

Drain tile & washed gravel relieve
hydrostatic pressure from retaining wall

Light colored
metal roofing
in warm climates

Solar Panels

R-30 + Insulation
Radiant Barrier

Arbor & covered porch
on east & west shelter
from hot summer sun

Deciduous vines over arbor and
windows allow for winter sunlight
to penetrate windows, yet block
summer sunlight from entering
the home

Summer Solstice Afternoon Sunlight Angle

Sunlight angles
vary with latitude.
Visit NOAA solar
position calculator
to find sun angles
for your latitude.

Winter Solstice afternoon sunlight @ 34 degrees 36'10' N

Pond for winter
sunlight reflection

Primary Garden Area
able to be flood irrigated
with pond --->

Passive Heating

24b Passive Cooling

Passive cooling is the process of using natural elements to keep a building cool in the summer including using shade and insulation to keep heat out, making use of geothermal principles (using the temperature of the Earth to cool a structure), and using evaporative cooling techniques.

Evaporative cooling occurs when water evaporates from a system. Buildings with a green roof should be watered in the morning. Energy from the sun will be absorbed by that water during the day and evaporate, resulting in a cooler building.

The following methods use geothermal principles. Please note the appropriate application will depend on your exact location.

If you can choose the location and design of your house, dig into the ground and create a basement or walkout basement. The earth will reduce the temperature to approximately 55 degrees.

Run a pipe through a body of water like a pond or lake or river, then pump the cold water through a heat exchange unit or a radiator similar to what is in your HVAC unit. A solar pump can then be used to circulate the water through the system.

The last method is to bury a long pipe allowing for air intake at one end while the other end opens into a structure. Open a window at the top of the structure. The hot air will exit, creating negative pressure in the building and pull cold air in through the buried pipe. If you cannot bury a pipe, you can achieve similar results by opening windows on the first floor; note that this works when the outside temperature is cooler than the inside temperature.

ACTION IDEAS

How could you implement passive cooling into your current situation? How about new construction? Make some sketches below.

Passive Cooling

25 Raise the Roof!

Your roof, as it stares up into the sky, represents a small area of the planet that once was nature. It was probably a forest, pasture, or garden, producing food and clean air while filtering water and housing millions of organisms. Unlike that original terrain, many roofs are made of asphalt shingles, which are usually dark in color and soak up heat from the sun. This heat makes it harder to keep the house cool. It also nearly eliminates a chance of survival for organisms within that area.

Consider creating a garden roof. Soil and plants together act as a great insulator. You may want to hire a professional for this, as your roof might be too steep, or not structurally supportive enough to carry the extra weight of a green roof. If we were to put gardens on top of all of the commercial roofs in America, this space alone might be enough to feed the population.

If you are not into living under your garden, installing light colored metal roofing can help keep you home cool in a warm climate. I prefer a light colored steel or aluminum roofing because it reflects a lot of heat, it usually lasts longer than shingles, and it is recyclable at the end of its life.

Urban landscapes have the potential to be very productive and quite sustainable. If your food is being produced in the same square footage as you are living or working, energy associated with shipping, transport, and refrigeration could be nearly eliminated.

ACTION ITEMS

Is your roof flat and strong enough to support a garden? If you live in an apartment building, can you talk to your landlord about the possibility of gardening on the roof?

Raise the Roof!

26 Plant Seeds

"If you are thinking for a year, plant rice. If you are thinking for ten years, plant a tree. If you are thinking for 100 years, teach children." ~Guan Zhong (7th Century BCE)

Seeds can be sown literally in the ground, or figuratively as great ideas in the minds of others. Both kinds of sowing are necessary to achieve sustainability. Practicing patience is important in this step. Plant annuals for immediate food production. Let some of the annuals completely mature, and collect their seeds for planting next year. Perennials are plants that live more than two years. Woody perennials are things like shrubs, trees, and vines that continue to grow in size every year and can provide fruits, nuts, bark, leaves, sap and building materials. Sow seeds in the ground and sow ideas in hearts and minds. Share the practice and knowledge of planting seeds with others.

Like me, you might not have much time for gardening. Given this constraint, I devised a method similar to what Masanobu Fukuoka calls the "do nothing method."

1. Gather several different kinds of seeds in bulk that are appropriate to plant for your season.
2. Mix them all up in a bag, and cast the seeds throughout the garden in areas where you think they will grow. Sometimes I throw them in other areas too, just to see what happens.
3. If you cast the seeds among weeds, wait a few days and then chop and drop the weeds.
4. Water is key, so if it's not raining on a regular, you may need to irrigate.

This method is not as effective as a light tillage of the soil followed by weeding and regular irrigation, but it is a fast and easy way to get started.

Growing perennials and woody perennial crops require less overall time investment because they come back year after year. Sometimes, I'll stick random seeds in the ground to see what happens, however seeds from these crops may be slightly more difficult to germinate as they sometimes require stratification and/or scarification in order to germinate. Still do not hesitate to plant them. The next generations will thank you.

Plant seeds for diversity. For the best results, plant crops that yield in different times of the year and in different locations (root crops, ground covers, low growing shrubs, under-story, vines, and over-story).

ACTION IDEAS

Where can you buy or obtain seeds that you can plant today?

Plant Seeds

27 Curb the Burn

To support our current comfortable lifestyle, we are burning too many non-renewable resources for our energy needs. According to the US Energy Information Administration (EIA), as of 2019, it was roughly 63% non renewable consisting of mostly coal, natural gas, propane, and crude oil. We have improved over the recent years, but this is still a reckless use of resources that continues to weaken the foundation for a civilization.

Unlike fossil fuels that were millions of years in the making, fuels from recently created organic matter, like wood, plants, and manures, are *renewable* resources.

If we burn renewable resources, we create a closed loop system. As a plant grows, it pulls carbon dioxide and other gases out of the atmosphere. Yes, the tree is actually made almost entirely from thin air. When burning wood, or other plant material, carbon dioxide returns to the atmosphere.

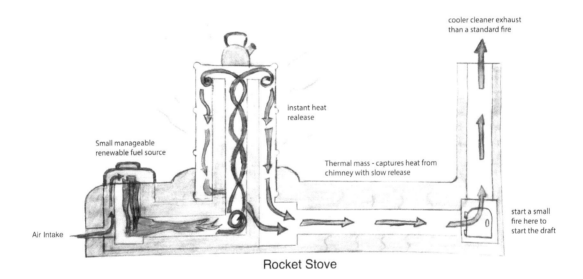

Rocket Stove

Be selective in the trees you harvest for fuel: choose dead trees over live and be conscious of the fact that even dead trees play an important ecological role as habitats for animals and fungi, plus the regeneration of soil. Use only what you need. Best practices include finding trees that are already down, or need to come down for safety reasons. Dead standing trees provide some of the driest wood, but keep an eye out for animals nesting in the hollows. Also, don't try to push over a dead tree. It's likely dead wood from the top will break out and fall on you. We could curb the wildfires if we implemented selective thinning practices and gathered fuels from the forest floor.

Rocket mass heaters are extremely efficient means of burning wood. The principle is simple: instead of burning large chunks of wood, rocket stoves burn sticks. Sticks have a higher surface area to volume ratio, so as the sticks heat up in the fire, more gas is released in the form of smoke. Airflow is directed over the small fire chamber, which causes most of the smoke to burn, which in turn produces more heat and less pollution. You can maximize the efficiency of a rocket mass system by collecting the heat from the chimney into a thermal mass, such as rocks, soil, bricks or water. The thermal mass will heat up, and maintain a steady release of heat even after the fire goes out. Therefore, whereas most heating stoves must burn a large quantity of wood continuously, a rocket mass heater achieves the same end result by burning for a short period of time with a smaller quantity of wood.

In addition to our energy, we should also consider how we "dispose" of our leaves, underbrush, and tree trimmings. Rather than burning this "waste," use it as mulch.

CHOP – DROP – MULCH – COVER

This allows the carbon sequestered from the organic matter to return and remain in the soil. Mulching also covers the soil that suppresses weeds, holds moisture and feeds the life of the surrounding plants.

In regards to using manure, besides burning the dry manure for fuel, another practical solution is to capture methane from commercial farms to supplement propane and natural gas needs. We could literally produce "crap loads" of methane if we just got our shit together.

ACTION IDEAS

28 5 S's of Water

Follow the 5 S's and watch miracles unfold

Water is life. Have you ever tried going more than a few days without it? This chapter will help you think about and manage the water in and around your home. The 5 S's of water represent a series of bio-intentional systems to filter and maximize water's potential. They have been in use for millennia (for example, Chinese rice fields), *but are often forgotten or ignored in the world of big agribusiness.* Try using these S's, in this order, if possible. This step will reduce the amount of water you need to purchase from municipalities, and improve the overall living systems.

1. **Slow it** - Following gravity, a drop of rain will fall once released from the cloud. Post impact, the drop of water will find the easiest way to the lowest point. Since water feeds life, if we begin the 5S's soon after impact, we can support more life. In doing this, we also reduce flash flooding issues down stream. Water can be slowed in a number of ways: through rain water collection, ponds, logs laid on contour, bales of straw, mulch, or other ground cover, such as grass, or forestry.

2. **Spread it** - Water has an amazing erosive capability. Too much water in one area can cause the land to rapidly degrade, losing valuable topsoil and sediments. Spreading water over the landscape will allow it more time to soak in. This can be achieved in a number of ways including sub-soiling, swales and berm construction, net and pan, or laying logs on contour.

3. **Soak it** - Soaking the water into the landscape will allow for the development of life in the soil in addition to the regeneration of aquifers, streams and rivers. Some of that water is **stored** in the soil to later evaporate forming cloud cover and a climate stability as well as feeding the plants, fungi, and microorganisms. This process happens naturally with healthy soils, however, when compact soils are an issue, slight loosening of the soil may be necessary. This can be achieved with a broad fork, shovels, one-time tillage, or cover crops.

4. **Store it** - In addition to water storage in soil and biomass, Easy small scale water storage can be accomplished with rain barrels and small ponds. Ponds and rain barrels can be used for hydro or aquaponics, and other aquatic food production in addition to watering plants.

And, they are home to many organisms that can benefit your garden such as mosquito eating fish like gambusia, frogs, tadpoles, and dragonflies.

5. **Share it** - You may find you have a surplus of stored water. Share it with your neighbor, or share it with your plants. The bounty of life is more enjoyable if we have someone to share it with.

ACTION IDEAS

How might you implement some of these S's into your life and living area?

5 S's of Water

29 A Journey to Paperless

Think of all of the ways in which we use paper, which mostly comes from trees: folders, files, receipts, junk mail, packaging, paper towels and toilet paper.

One day as I was fumbling through my office supplies looking for a folder to put all of my clients' information in, I thought, why print off all of the papers, buy the folders, paper, and ink, and store it in my filing cabinet when I could use the computer instead? I wasn't surprised to learn that, on average, about 50% of a company's waste is from paper products. I find it way easier to have all info on my computer or the cloud, plus use e-statements and paperless receipts. It's way less hassle to store and keep up with the records. Of course, the computer and the power to run it has a carbon footprint as well, but overall efficiency is greatly improved from using paper.

As for junk mail, how much do you get? For me, it was more than half of my mail. The most effective way to cancel is to call the company directly. Those companies are spending money to send out these advertisements, and they are usually glad to remove you from their mailing list on request. If you get a lot of junk mail, it could take a long time to contact each individual company, so here are a few websites to speed up the process: http://www.directmail.com/mail_preference, http://www.ecofuture.org, or if you need help finding links, visit our website at 71Solutions.org

Since online shopping will soon dominate the industry, we need to stay conscious of the packaging. An easy hack is to order more things at a time so they put 3 or 4 things into a huge box rather than just one. If available, always take advantage of green shipping options like USPS Blue Earth, FedEx, EarthSmart, or UPS Eco Responsible Packaging Program. Recycle boxes and envelopes, and use natural fibers for packing. If you don't recycle the paper and cardboard, you can use the products as sheet mulch.

Other ways of saving paper include using cloth towels or loofa instead of paper towels and handkerchiefs instead of facial tissues. If you have to buy paper towels, try recycled paper towels, or something with a smaller carbon footprint, like bamboo. Also, keep an eye out for hemp, banana, or another means of quickly renewable resources and agricultural byproducts. Some people have installed a bidet and moved away from toilet paper completely; however managing water resources is important too, especially in an arid or semiarid environment. We have mullein growing wild, and the leaves happen to make a great toilet paper substitute. It is also said to be medicinal for respiratory issues. Mullein is a plant that you may find beneficial in the event of another pandemic because we all know someone is going to hoard the TP.

ACTION IDEAS

What is one strategy for going paperless that you can commit to implementing this week?

A Journey to Paperless

30 Yards to Gardens

"You can spend your whole life traveling around the world searching for the Garden of Eden, or you can create it in your backyard." - Khang Kijarro Nguyen

Is your yard consuming more than it is producing? Do you ever wonder why we have lawns to begin with? These massive grassy areas usually originated either as a symbol of wealth, a play space, or for grazing livestock. Now, even the poorest among us have lawns. Many are never used for play, and there is no livestock in sight.

Lawns consume money and time which, to me are both extremely valuable resources, and they do not usually produce much of anything except, for some, the idea of "nice." To me, nice is having a shady space that produces food, income, and freedom.

Some people choose to transition their lawns into a native species sanctuary, which is great for wildlife in addition to being low maintenance. If we take it a step further and plant food, medicine, pollinators, and support species in our lawns, our front yard suddenly becomes a pantry, pharmacy, and wildlife sanctuary. In addition, by growing food at home, you preserve other wild habitats from future destruction in the name of agriculture. If you don't want to plant annuals, consider perennials and woody vines, bushes, and trees. A mature perennial system can be extremely low maintenance.

If you are unsure of what to plant, or how to do it most effectively, search for permaculture designers or edible landscaping professionals in your area. You may also want to check out my class, "Grow Food and Medicine: Helping Busy People Build Resilience" at Mastermind.com. Well planned and planted, your property will be "good for food and pleasing to the eye" (Genesis 3:6). When installing a garden in your yard, listen to nature. You will have pests and diseases, especially in the first years as the ecosystem develops. Eventually, a balance will occur, but only if you observe and interact appropriately. The plants that do not survive and thrive will be replaced with more resilient species. Also, be sure to plan your garden around the **5 S's** of water.

For us, some common vegetables do not do well without inputs, but here are a few that do: peas, kale, okra, beans, figs, blueberries, kiwi, persimmons, blackberries, sage, rosemary, elderberry, maypop (aka passion flower/fruit) and mints are all prolific with low input other than harvesting, occasional pruning, and the initial installation. This, of course, will vary by location.

ACTION IDEAS

Besides an expensive and time-consuming symbol of wealth, what could you transform your yard into?

What are some crops that do well without much input in your particular location?

31 Know Your Farmer

*"Whatever lofty things you might accomplish today,
you will do them only because you first ate something that grew out of dirt."*
~Barbara Kingsolver, Author

Meet your local holistic farmers, and buy from them. Find them through organized farm tours and nearby farmers markets, produce stands or, of course, search the internet.

It is important to research the quality of food and find farmers who grow ethically. I encourage you to go beyond organic. The "organic" certification is a good start, but holistically managed farms that are not necessarily "organic certified" often far exceed the criteria of the "organic." What do you do if you simply can't find holistic foods, locally grown without toxic pesticides? Make it known to your local farmers that there is demand for it, and maybe you can help change your local market.

Some farms will sell directly to you, which will get you some of the freshest food available and create a beneficial relationship with your neighbors. Shopping locally also helps to build your community. If you buy local food, you keep the money in the local economy and you also reduce the amount of energy expended on food transportation.

One last idea: you could be the farmer! Check out Joel Salatin's 1998 book, *You Can Farm*. If you want a little hands-on experience before you jump into farming, check out WWOOF.org for World Wide Opportunities on Organic Farms.

ACTION IDEAS

List 5 holistic farmers in your area. Would you consider being a farmer?

Know Your Farmer

32 Patterns First, Then Details
A David Holmgren Permaculture Principle

As you work toward resilience and sustainability in your life, don't get too bogged down in the details. Before taking any new major step, it is good to first step back and examine the overarching patterns.

Consider your long-term vision against more immediate needs and desires, then look at your available resources. It's also important to consider what feeds your body and soul. You might consider the lists you created in **Value Yourself** and **Identify Assets & Minimize Liabilities**. Which of your needs and desires are easily met, and which will require a lot of additional resources?

When the Seneca Treehouse Project began, I did not know where it would end up. I knew that we needed to live more sustainably (the pattern), but I did not know that it would end up being an intentional community and permaculture learning center for eco-tourism (the detail). I also knew that we needed to grow more food (the pattern), but I had no experience in gardening or farming at the time, and so I had no idea of what exactly I wanted to grow (the detail). I decided to get chickens for eggs and to add fertility to the land (the pattern), but I didn't know exactly what breed to get, how many birds, or where the best place to put them on the land (the detail).

As we develop Treehouse Internatural, we keep in mind the primary focus on education (the pattern) in order to develop a curriculum to fit the needs of the people through the changing times (the details). Once the patterns are established, it's easier to determine the details, and the details are easy to change.

ACTION IDEAS

What details are you getting stuck on? What are some of the bigger picture patterns to start with?

Patterns First, Then Details

33 Use Appropriate Technology & Use Technology Appropriately

Appropriate technology is that which is small scale and attainable by the average individual to produce basic necessities. This may vary by location. Appropriate technology uses less energy or is powered by human or animal energy, and is usually built using either natural, recycled, or commonly available materials. A few examples of appropriate technology are things like a bicycle, pedal powered generators or pumps and washing machines, A-frame level or a water level, chicken tractors, and of course hand tools like shovels and trowels.

One disadvantage to appropriate technology is that it usually takes more time. If you choose to use the alternative, advanced technology, use it wisely. Technology can be fruitful, or wasteful, depending on how you use it. For instance, the internet provides us with access to much of the world's knowledge, which we can use to improve our society, or waste our lives. We can use it for good energy and healing, or to troll social media and pick fights with people.

Personally, I use a lot of advanced technology, and I try to remain conscious about the time I save in doing so. Using this technology frees me up to do more of what I enjoy.

Bicycles are a perfect example of appropriate technology. However, most of the time, I don't have an option to ride a bike. I can't haul 4000 lbs worth of tools and building materials with my bicycle. I can, however, purchase biodiesel to fuel my truck and practice the 5 R's when it breaks.

I also use a mini excavator. Before I purchased it, I weighed the pros and cons. And I did the experiment: I hired people to dig and did a lot of digging myself. I realized how expensive it was, and how sore we were after a day of digging. I purchased the machine primarily for restoration and agriculture purposes like installing ponds and swales, moving logs, and planting trees. I also use it for digging foundations, septic systems, and greywater systems. One gallon of diesel equates to about 100 man-hours. Now I can hire people to do work that is healthier for them, which leads to more happiness and we can do more good elsewhere.

My vision and hope for humanity is, in essence, using appropriate technology wherever feasible and advanced technology to increase wisdom and explore new and exciting things under our feet and in the stars. Using appropriate technology and using technology appropriately also frees up time that we can then spend with the people we love in addition to reducing the cost of living. This will increase the accessibility of basic necessities for all people and improve businesses, homesteads, communities, and ecosystems globally.

ACTION IDEAS

Where can you use more appropriate technology? How can you use technology more appropriately and what would you do with the extra time?

Use Appropriate Technology & Use Technology Appropriately

34 Drive Smart

Cars may not be the symbol of personal freedom we once thought they were. Sure, they let us go wherever we want, whenever we want to. But the convenience of cheap gas has led to a culture of instant gratification and a sense of urgency to go fulfill our wishes *immediately*, sometimes by driving to buy one thing at a time, and often doing it alone.

The price we pay for fuel doesn't reflect its actual cost. It is heavily subsidized by military expenditures and other tax related services. In a sense, we are buying oil on environmental and cultural credit, as we will be paying for the effects of oil extraction well into the future. You may not be able to alter the policy behind oil production, but you *can* take steps right now to change the way you rely on this very expensive substance. Before you get in your car, ask yourself:

1. Do I really need to do this now or can it wait?
2. Can I walk or ride a bike instead of driving?
3. What else can I accomplish while I am out?
4. Can I carpool, or run errands with someone else who needs to go? If you have a smartphone, search for carpooling apps.
5. Can I take public transportation?
6. What is the most efficient route?

ACTION IDEAS

What is one recommendation for "driving smart" that you can commit to implementing this week?

Drive Smart

35 Bike for Abundance

"I don't ride a bike to add days to my life. I ride a bike to add life to my days"
– Unknown

Riding a bike is fun, healthy, and you get to see a lot more of your surroundings than when you're bookin' it down the road in a big chunk of metal, watching the dotted line dash pass.

Bike travel is slower, and can be dangerous, especially if your city hasn't made any room on busy roads for bikes. Safety is key, so make sure you wear a helmet. Stay alert to traffic and if you're listening to music, keep one ear open to your surroundings.

I have a friend that used to ride 22 miles round trip to school and back nearly every day. How many miles do you cover daily on the way to work, school or shopping? How much money do you spend on gas, and on a gym membership? Think of the gas you can save, the muscles you can build and the calories you can burn on a bike.

While you embark on this endeavor, think about some other tangential benefits that could be associated with biking instead of driving. Maybe you could bring awareness to biking by meeting your legislators, and request road signs for safety. Or by organizing biking outings.

The idea of "biking for abundance" came to me on my bike during a journey from Maine to Rhode Island. The idea is to form a group of people, plot a trip, and add value to the land and communities that you pass along the way by planting seeds and offering services. I learned that groups are already out there doing something similar. There might be such a group near you. Fleet Farming, from Orlando, Florida is one of those groups. Basically, they use urban land and other people's lawns to farm and produce local food, and they do it on bikes!

ACTION IDEAS

How could biking add abundance in your life?

Bike for Abundance

36 EAT - Energizing, Alkalizing & Tasty - Food
"Let Food Be Thy Medicine, and Medicine Be Thy Food" ~Hippocrates

EAT food! Energizing, Alkalizing & Tasty Food. Try to eat a variety of different colors (search the internet for "nutrition by color" images) in order to get the balanced diet needed to stay firm against disease and aging. The food you eat also has an effect on your blood pH. Your ideal blood pH is around 7.3, which is slightly alkalized. Foods like processed sugar, bleached flour, coffee, soda, and meat are all very common in the average American's diet, and also happen to be acid-forming, which can lead to disease. Consider early human populations and indigenous peoples who still live in the wild. Their diets consist of of greens, grains, flowers, herbs, nuts, mushrooms, fruits and meat. Most of these foods tend to be alkalizing, expecially when consumed as whole foods.

We who live in "developed" countries must also be aware of the food additives (see **Read the Label**). The U.S. allows food additives that are illegal in other developed countries. They are illegal in those countries because they are bad for you! Read the labels on foods, and look up the words you don't know. As a simple rule, go around the perimeter of the grocery store to pick your groceries. This is where you can find the freshest and least processed foods.

Other tips for eating healthy can be found in **Read the Label** and **Know Your Farmer**. And remember, you can also grow it yourself!

ACTION IDEAS

Eating healthier can seem daunting unless you break it into smaller goals. Can you commit to eating closer to the earth for just one day/week?

EAT - Energizing, Alkalizing & Tasty - Food

37 Move Your Body

"Move your body, change your mind" ~Rachel Hollis

Call it work, exercise, sports, recreation, or using the handheld can opener instead of the electric one. The point here is to move your body. Sometimes I have a hard time fitting in exercise, but if I can accomplish a task while getting fit, then I am all in. The term "farm fitness" refers to using random things around the farm to get fit. My friend Chance would do lunges while carrying buckets of compost & other nuggets of nutrition. Sometimes, I like to go for a mushroom hunt run. Maybe we can call that one "forage fitness."

As a builder, I do a lot of moving my body. At 155 lbs, my greatest challenge is keeping my body strong enough to be effective with my work, and reduce my likelihood of injury. As I grow older, I am feeling more of a need to get aerobic workout in to get my blood flowing, keep my brain sharp, and flush out toxins. Listen to your body and do what is best for it. It may be different for everyone depending on your needs, age, and current physical condition.

Getting regular exercise can be a challenging habbit to form. If you are an extrovert, you many find it easier to workout with someone else, or even a group of people. As someone who was not born into a habit of working out, I love having a personal trainer to tell me where I am messing up, or what I can do better. If you are new to exercising, you may feel a bit sick once you begin. Drink lots of water, stretch, and keep going. It will get better.

You really don't need to dedicate long hours to exercising. You might try a 10-minute HIIT (High Intensity Interval Training). You can download apps that times out each round with a 10-20 second break in between. Including the stretches prior to the workout, it amounts to about 15 minutes of time. This is something the whole family can get involved in. My son Abel likes to climb on my back when I'm doing pushups, and we sometimes hold the baby while doing squats. Who needs weights and a gym membership when you have kids and a farm?

If all of that sounds too intense, you could try dancing, swimming, walking, yoga, canoing, or hiking. Anything to get the body moving and keep the blod flowing.

ACTION IDEAS

What are some ways you can add more movement to your life throughout the day?

Move Your Body

38 Raise Animals with a Purpose

Beginning about 15,000 years ago, humans began domesticating animals as companions, as food, and as assistants in work.

A lot of animals can eat plants and insects that we would not normally want to, or be able to digest. This is one way to turn those products into food for us. I know… a touchy subject in today's society. But even if you are a vegetarian or a vegan, animals — as beloved pets and helpers — can still assist you in the garden through pest reduction and nutrients production. In a holistically managed farm system, whether vegetarian or not, the animals often live a healthy and happy life.

Try not to have animals that will break your bank if you don't have enough land to produce their food. If you have animals and do not consume meat, you will have to separate or castrate to keep from overpopulating. Keep in mind how much food the animal will consume. We supplement our chicken feed through compost, insects, and weeds, none of which I want to eat, but the chickens love it! Our chickens run around all day, eat insects and sleep in the trees.

When considering raising animals, give some thought to the problems and questions of ethical husbandry. Keep your animals comfortable, happy and healthy. If they have something to do whether it's fetching a stick, herding other animals, or searching for food, they are likely to be happier and healthier.

ACTION IDEAS

Raise Animals with a Purpose

39 Polyculture Systems

"It is time for parents to teach young people early on that in diversity there is beauty and there is strength." ~Maya Angelou, Author

The majority of the plant and animal-based goods that are consumed today are produced in a monoculture system. In other words, one single species is grown on a massive scale. It is done this way largely due to the economy of scale. The more of one thing you do, the cheaper it becomes per unit. One major dark side to this trade-off is disease. If you have seven acres of corn, and a disease strikes, your entire crop could easily be lost. The other financial issue is in the amount of insurance a farmer needs to buy in order to protect the one vulnerable species. If you raise a diversified crop instead, say one acre each of corn, beets, beans, rice, trees, vines, and shrubs, then the corn might be lost, but the rest may likely survive. It's also possible that the other crops can form a balanced ecosystem, strengthening the system as a whole, reducing or eliminating the disease all together.

Observing nature at work in the wild, you will rarely, if ever find a monoculture. Rather, you will see numerous species, all thriving together. They support one another in various ways, and they fill a niche in time and in space. Modeling nature's intricacy, you can have root crops growing with ground covers, vines, bushes, and trees all in one space. They will produce at different times of the year providing balanced nutrition and an abundance of food. One disease or pest is not likely to take out your entire food system. Add perennials and woody crops which are often less work inputs than annuals. Add ponds, berms and swales into your earthworks and the issue of flooding and droughts will be reduced. Add animals into the system and you will have pest control and increased fertilization, reducing the external inputs required to meet those needs. And, you can attract beneficial insects, reptiles, and amphibians through the development of polyculture ecosystems all the while creating less work and more beautification for you.

ACTION IDEAS

How can you promote polyculture systems in your living area?

Polyculture Systems

40 Seek a Mentor/Be a Mentor

"A smart person learns from their own mistakes, a wise person learns from others."

When I learned about Scott Niswonger's vision to "learn, earn and return," it resonated with me. I find that applying this to the people that I spend time with helps me to maximize my potential and quality of life.

While there is value in learning before you earn and return, and many people might think that returning is for their end years, the reality is that we learn, earn and return our whole lives. Older brother teaches younger brother how to tie his shoelaces; Dad teaches daughter how to bake a cake; student teaches teacher about the latest i-device; have-nots teach the affluent about the power of giving; and television presents viewers with inspirational people, from the very young to the very old. Whether you're a professional teacher or a self-professed life-long learner, give some consideration to how you spend your learning, earning and returning time and strive for a balance.

Learn - Spend 1/3 of your time with mentors (in person, YouTube, teachers, books)

Earn - Spend 1/3 of your time with peers (friends, coworkers, family)

Return - Spend 1/3 of your time helping (as a mentor, with young people, volunteering)

A mentor-mentee relationship can be formal or informal, tacit or expressed, geographically close or distant. When considering mentors, seek people who are experts in their fields and have skills in areas you would like to grow. Strive for at least one personal mentor that will give you direct feedback and accountability. Also, no matter your age, be open to the possibility of someone wanting YOU as a mentor.

ACTION IDEAS

Who are some people in my life currently that I can learn from? Who, or how could I be a mentor in my community?

Seek a Mentor/Be a Mentor

41 Learn Another Language

"Building bridges is the best defence against ignorance." ~Aaron Lauritsen, Author

There has never been, nor will there ever likely be, a universal language. What if the brain is like an ecosystem, teeming with variety, potential, diversity, complexity? What happens when we force it to think, speak and express itself in just one way? This is monolingualism, the epitome of a "first world problem." According to Ethnologue, there are 7,117 languages in the world. Language lives in diversity. Language *is* diversity. That's why learning another language is like striking at the root of monoculture. It's not just about acquiring one more marketable skill, it's about being able to speak and understand a different culture in its own terms, and opening up your mind to another way of seeing and saying the world.

Language, simply put, is a method of communication. I know that learning a foreign language is not something that can be knocked out in a weekend or even a couple of weeks. Another type of language that I believe is even more important to start with is the language of love.

Learning the love languages will help you have a deeper appreciation and understanding of the subcultures within your own language. As Gary Chapman talks about in his *Five Love Languages* series, we all have different means of communicating and expressing ourselves within and without our words. We can speak the same language as someone else, but fail to communicate if we don't know whom we're talking to and how to choose and order our words. The love languages started as a means of learning about your significant other, but the concept can be applied to any situation. Some people really like words of affirmation; others prefer direct feedback. And the languages are interwoven. For instance. I highly value acts of service, but I do not like gifts, unless that is, the gift is an act of service. Gifts I like are pragmatic gifts, things that I can use or eat, or use to build something.

Similar to love languages, there are several personality-testing sites out there to get to know yourself, and your community even better. The Enneagram, DISC and 16 personalities, formerly known as "Myers Briggs" are some common test types that will reveal so much about building better relationships with your peers. If you are butting heads with your partner, or just want to take a relationship to a new level, try learning the different personality types and how to communicate with each other. It's not exactly learning a foreign language, but it is a good way to broaden your native touch.

Learning another language does more than break down borders; it helps you appreciate differences and build a better community.

ACTION IDEAS

Take a few minutes to reflect on this information, about breaking down borders, about opening yourself up to communication, about being more inclusive. What languages can I begin learning (foreign or otherwise) in order to build bridges and strengthen community?

Learn Another Language

42 Hang Out the Laundry

According to *USA Today*, Americans spend about $4 billion per year to dry their clothes. That does not include the cost of the dryer and dryer sheets. And did you know that known carcinogens have been found in certain dryer sheet brands? Even smelling the added scents can be harmful if they are not natural, and wearing the clothes on your skin can do damage as well.

Hanging your clothes outside can be a nice way to appreciate the outdoors and be with nature. Sometimes the clothes become a bit crispy when hung out to dry. Using less detergent will reduce the stiffness, and consequently save you money on detergent. For guests staying in our bed & breakfast, we often line dry, and then throw them in the dryer for a few minutes to fluff them up a bit for added comfort.

Hanging out the clothes is slower and can be counter-productive on a rainy day. In the cold winter, we use the dryer more, and we divert the dryer exhaust into the house through a lint trap. This adds moisture to the air, so we monitor the humidity to ensure it is not too much. Do not ventilate inside if you have a gas dryer; the exhaust will have carbon monoxide in it.

ACTION IDEAS

What is the best area outside my home where I can install a clothesline?

Hang Out the Laundry

43 Simplify: Take the Best and Leave the Rest

"You can do everything; you just can't do it all at once."
~Thomas J. Bunn, Scott's dad

We are complex creatures. It is easy for us to get involved in many things. I used to make lists upon lists of things that I "needed" to do. It was usually in the form of sticky notes pasted in random places. It wasn't until simplifying that it all began to flow.

Start with a few simple adjustments to simplify your life and work right away:

- Reduce steps between one place and another, especially between places you visit often.
- Edit your emails and messages for efficiency. Cal Newport's book *Deep Work* has a great chapter on simplifying your textual interactions called "Drain the Shallows."
- Simplify your workspace and eliminate distractions
- Silence your phone when focusing on a task
- Turn off social media notifications - set a time to check them, rather than looking every time your phone tells you to.

- Learn to say **NO** more often so that you can say **YES** to what is most important.

I suggest creating a mission and vision statement. This is the what, why, and sometimes how of your intention. See chapter **70 - Stick to the List**, for more details.

Sometimes you might find you need to complicate things before you can simplify. For example, if you're faced with a complex problem, it's often helpful to first spill everything out on the table, brainstorm without limit, and *then* simplify: select the elements that are most important or urgent to you, and get rid of the rest (at least for the moment).

Suggested readings: *The One Thing* by Gary Keller; *Deep Work* by Cal Newport

ACTION IDEAS

What are some activities going on in your life right now that could be simplified using some of the given suggestions?

44 Ask Questions

Asking = As King: *Always continue asking as a good king would do.*

It feels nice to be right. While it doesn't usually feel so nice to be wrong, being wrong is a great way to grow. Because being wrong feels so crummy, it is often the best way to learn and retain new information. Sometimes though, there is no right and wrong, but only opinion. Rather than being upset at the other person's opinion, you can ask questions to see their viewpoint.

At one point in time, most humans thought the earth was flat. Now we know that it is not. Currently most of humanity agrees that it is a sphere, but that's not quite true either. It is spherical, but it's not a perfect sphere. It bulges slightly at the equator due to the centrifugal force of the rotation.

No matter how much you think you know, never stop asking questions. Some questions may be a good reminder of what we don't want in our lives. Good leaders listen to what people want, what's most important, and what fuels the passion.

In today's political environment, it's so easy to get emotionally outraged when we disagree. When in disagreement, seek to truly understand. In reality, very little is black and white. It is important to listen completely to the answer and maintain humility. In other words, listen to get it and not to reply.

ACTION IDEAS

Who is someone in your life you don't see eye-to-eye with? What questions might you ask them next time you meet in order to build greater understanding between the two of you?

Ask Questions

45 Respect Your Neighbor

The average American neighborhood has lost its community connectivity. Where we buy or build our homes is so often determined by school districts, job opportunities, curb appeal or geographical location. Seldom do we settle somewhere because of who lives next door, or just down the road. Yet these are the people we end up seeing, hearing, and often being with on a daily basis. It is our neighbors that can make living in a place wonderful, or terrible, and we often do not get to choose whom we live next to.

Take my example. I built a house on the lake when I was in college. I had no sense of sustainability in mind at the time, and gave no real concern to the fact that the site was right next to an RV park. Thirteen years later, even though I love them, my neighbors often drive me crazy! Barking dogs, non-shop mowers, blowers, and weed eaters. On the flip side, all of my neighbors have had to put up with ME over the years with my late night parties when I was in college, to my obnoxious dogs, guineas and roosters, midnight metal fabrication projects, and building materials sitting everywhere.

At least two avenues exist for improving the quality of a neighborhood. One is to take control and choose to live in an intentional community. The other is to surrender and accept. Build on common ground and agree to disagree.

One way to bring your neighborhood together is to build an ARK - to do Acts of Random Kindness. Here are a few ideas:

- Plant fruit and nut trees in the neighborhood
- Help the older neighbors with some chores
- Help watch and mentor the neighbors kids
- Create or participate in neighborhood events
- Share tools, materials and labor.

Next time you buy or build, spend more time getting to know your future potential neighbors. If you are already settled, try to get to know the ones you have.

There's gotta be an app for that!

ACTION IDEAS

What next steps can you take to get to know your neighbors better? What random acts of kindness can you do for them?

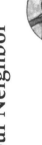

Respect Your Neighbor

46 Multitask

Look up the term "multitask," and you will find that it was created to describe a computer's ability to do multiple tasks at once. Computers are very good at this at some level, but what happens when you try to download multiple big files at one time while streaming the latest *Game of Thrones* episode? You may notice, as your bandwidth gets eaten up, that your download progress bar petrifies and the beautiful, high-definition faces on the screen start to look like 1980's computer graphic technology. Something similar happens in our brain's brain.

We can only process so much at one time. Take on too many simultaneous tasks, and you end up dividing your focus, usually compromising quality and effectiveness. Why then are we encouraged to multitask so much? Well, there are effective and ineffective ways of doing it, and it may not be for everyone.

An ineffective way to multitask is to try to do too many *of the same kinds of things* at once. IF you are proficient at multiple tasks, IF they are different kinds of tasks that do not require the same part of your brain and IF they are not extremely critical tasks, then multitasking can help you do more with less time. An effective way to multitask is to pair complementary tasks, like something active with something passive, or something physical with something mental. Here are a few suggestions:

Take a moment for meditation or mindfulness while you're on the bus or train

- Do some yoga while you're on the phone
- Listen to podcasts or audiobooks while doing repetitive tasks, driving, or perhaps on a tractor.
- Create an exercise routine out of repetitive physical labor
- Wisely read or write while in a bus, on a train, or riding in a car.
- Babysitting exercise (squats while holding baby, pulling the kids around in a bike trailer, or other means of using the kiddos as weights.)

If you form a routine of doing these things, you can either free up time in your life, or fit in more. At this point in my life, I tend to prefer the latter.

ACTION IDEAS

What can you do to multitask without compromising quality of life or quality of the task? Would you prefer to have more time to relax, or fit more into your life? What have you been multitasking at that you probably shouldn't?

Multitask

47 Honor the Greater Good

God, Great Spirit, Allah, The Force, The Universe, Buddha, the Tao. These terms all represent humanity's enduring desire to name a guiding force in all of our lives. These names, however are ultimately imperfect, and have caused great separation, bloodshed, and war. Despite their differences, they all have one thing in common. These Names all reach toward understanding something that is greater than us – the whole of which every individual person and thing is included.

You, I, and everyone you have ever known are inseparable from this greatness. Your body is made of the same particles of which our planet is made. We were born and we shall die in this universe. We never were and never will be separate. Take a few minutes every day to honor the greater good. Be in the attitude of gratitude for all you have, and all of the opportunities.

Create your own thoughts, prayers, affirmations, or incantations that work for you. Mine varies a lot, but here is a standard go-to:

"Thank you for this life, my family and these friends. Thank you for my place in this world. Help me to be an instrument of good will, and guide me to be the best that I can be.

ACTION IDEAS

What are 5-10 things that you are grateful for? How could you honor the greater good and implement the attitude of gratitude in your daily life?

Honor the Greater Good

48 Build Confidence

For the longest time, I didn't realize all of the self-talk that was going on in my head. For me, much of that was ruled by the fear of what other people thought of me. Then I figured out that everyone else was thinking the same thing! Looking at it that way, it's easier to see that you are just as cool as they are. Those who may pick on you are simply afraid of you or insecure about themselves, therefore need to put someone down in order to feel better about themselves. Put that way, it almost makes you feel sorry for them.

But don't worry about what everyone else thinks. Follow your heart and simply do what feeds you. This is where extraordinary things happen. The more you put yourself out there, the more results you will see. Know that for everyone who is being ill towards you, at least one other person is willing you forward.

If you are not confident in something, it may be because you don't have the skills to do it. So work on building the skills!

Throughout my career, I have had many clients ask me if I could do something. If I didn't know how, I would figure it out with the help of the internet and picking the brains of other professionals. The next step is to try, and expect to fail a few times. If you don't give up, you will eventually get it right, and build confidence. The more skills you have, the more confident you become.

Also, consider lessons from other chapters like, **Focus on the Light** and **Honor the Greater Good**, and **Learn a Trade** to assist in buiding confidence.

ACTION IDEAS

What are some skills you can work on honing this week in order to build up your confidence? What are some things you can tell yourself to build confidence?

Build Confidence

49 Maintain Integrity

Integrity, by definition, is the state of being whole or undivided as well as being honest and having strong moral principles. Everyone has a different moral compass that directs their sense of integrity. Always strive to be the best you can be. Integrity is not something anyone achieves entirely all at once because entropy, the gradual decline to disorder, is constantly at work on integrity. Maintaining integrity is a process of building and rebuilding through the journey of life. You don't just get it and have it forever.

Consider the following in situations where integrity is lacking.

First, address the issue: what went wrong? is an apology necessary?

Then comes the repair: If something is broken, fix it and then do your best not to do it again, by whatever means necessary.

Example

Address the issue: I wrecked your car

The Fix: I will make the repairs necessary and pay for a rental car while yours is being fixed.

Realizing we've made a mistake and confessing to it can be scary, especially if we think those we have affected may be angry. If we don't have the skills or resources to fix a mistake, this can be even more intimidating. Stay strong and push forth anyway. Living a life with integrity makes you more trustworthy, helps you build better relationships, and allows you to be at peace with yourself.

We can expand the scope of integrity: consider the example of one person's trash in the city's drinking water. Whether or not it was intentionally polluted or who did it is beside the point. The point is to restore and maintain the integrity for the betterment of the whole. Integrity is about making the world a better place.

ACTION IDEAS

Are there any issues in your life where you feel the need to restore integrity? What things can you do to maintain integrity?

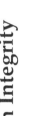

Maintain Integrity

50 Less Meat, More Mushrooms

We have all heard that factory meat farming is compromising the environment. In addition to buying locally and ethically raised meat, there is another solution to provide a taste-alike, and, of course, a vegetarian alternative to meat. Even though mushrooms do not provide as much protein and vitamin B12, they are full of nutritional benefits. They are medicinal and have been known to assist in the strategies for treating cancer, inflammation, high blood pressure, fatigue, and hormonal imbalances. They are also a general immune booster.

Mushrooms can be found in the grocery or farmers markets, however they are often somewhat expensive. You can also learn to forage, cultivate, or support local growers. If you want to hunt mushrooms, consider joining a club who can help you identify mushrooms that are edible and those that are toxic. Check out NAMYCO.org for a state-by-state list of clubs. Remember, "There are old mycologists and there are bold mycologists, but there are no old and bold mycologists." If you want to learn more about cultivating your own mushrooms, check out Tradd Cotter's book, *Organic Mushroom Farming & Mycoremediation* (Chelsea Green, 2014).

Mushrooms, like people, require oxygen to grow and produce carbon dioxide; their entire body of the mycelium is their "lungs." You can cultivate mushrooms in the garden, where a natural carbon oxygen exchange between plants and mushrooms occurs. If growing for production, a controlled environment would be better for minimizing insects and optimizing light, humidity, and gas exchange. Mycelium, the "roots" or filamentous vegetative growth of mushrooms, are also key to soil life stability, plant health, and water filtration.

In the southeastern United States, the following mushrooms are a few of my personal favorites to grow and find in the wild. They taste great sautéed with butter or coconut oil and garlic and salt.

Oyster – Raw, I think they smell a bit fishy, and when cooked, they taste amazing.

Lion's Mane – These are easy to identify, good for your nervous system, and have a unique taste that also somewhat resembles crabmeat or lobster.

Shiitake – These are similar in texture and can be seasoned like a steak.

Chicken of the Woods – You guessed it: their taste and texture when boiled and seasoned resembles chicken.

Chanterelles – Super easy to find and one of my favorites, although personally I can't say they taste like a certain meat.

King Oyster - A larger cousin of the native oysters, these are thick stemmed and tender. They are terrestrial and can be grown near queen ann's lace or carrots. The stems look and taste very much like scallops.

* Before you eat any mushroom you have collected, make sure your identification is 100% correct.

Enjoy and live strong.

ACTION IDEAS

What are some of your favorite recipes in which you could swap in mushrooms instead of meat?

Less Meat, More Mushrooms

51 Learn a Trade

A trade is any type of productive skill that requires more than just a few hours of training. Once you learn a trade, you will have it forever. Carpentry, weaving, welding, visual arts, and culinary arts are all examples trades. Personally, I am a jack of many trades. It has served me well so far and empowered me to thrive even through economic recessions.

How do you find a trade? Refer to the first chapter of this book. What do you like to do? Perhaps you don't know because you have never had the opportunity to try a trade before. That's ok, because the good news is that right *now* is the perfect time to start!

There are schools and work opportunities where you can gain experience in different trades to see if you like them. The Seneca Treehouse Project is a host farm listed with World Wide Opportunities on Organic Farms (WWOOF) where you can learn about construction, permaculture, self-development and business management. You can learn about other farms and the opportunities they offer at www.WWOOF.net.

You can even sample a trade by watching tutorial videos online. If your trade is programming, you don't have to get up from your desk and you can begin immediately. If you don't like it, just keep trying. Be aware, when you learn a trade, some aspects may not be enjoyable. This is a necessary part of the trade, so don't be discouraged just because you don't like a small part.

Once you have found a trade that you enjoy, check out trade shows and conventions, or online groups. Suppliers usually know a lot of tricks of the trade too. Keep it fresh by doing it often, and welcome the mistakes. Many of our students get discouraged because they don't want to make a mistake. After 25 years of building things, I could fill a book with all the mistakes I have made. As my dad would say, "Every carpenter makes mistakes. A good carpenter knows how to fix their mistakes." and that applies to all trades. The road to mastery is paved with mistakes. This solution is the reason I started Treehouse Trade School: to help people find confidence and abundance through skill training, team building, and sustainable community development.

ACTION IDEAS

Based on your interests and the exercises you've completed from prior chapters, which trade do you think you would most like to learn?

Learn a Trade

52 Prepare for Emergencies

What will you do if the power goes out for a week? What if the grocery store runs out of food? What if the gas stations run dry, or you get fired? What if you get injured or sick? Are you prepared? These sorts of questions, or worse, run through everyone's mind from time to time, and it is easy to dwell on disaster scenarios to the point of anxiety. That's why the most common reaction to thinking about emergencies is probably to "snap out of it" and ignore the inner prepper.

It's a waste of time to worry about futures you cannot control, and it is also a bad idea to presuppose that present comforts will always be there, and to ignore the real possibility of change, adversity, and hardship. In between these extremes is room for a healthy attitude toward the possibility of change, as conserved in the Boy Scout's motto, "Be Prepared."

As of April 15th, 2020, my hometown was in a state of emergency. COVID 19 caused many people to lose their jobs. People were sick or paranoid about becoming ill. The grocery stores were slim on supplies. Then, a tornado hit the city, and people were out of power. The gas stations were not able to pump gas, in addition to being out of ice, and trees were covering the roads. People were forced to get out and work together in the midst of a social distancing pandemic.

Here are some basic recommendations to prepare for emergencies:

- Have enough food stored for a minimum of 30 days. Rotate it out so it doesn't go bad.
- Have enough money in your savings to pay for 3 months of being out of work plus your health insurance deductible, in case you happen to get injured.
- Be prepared to use a bicycle or livestock for transporting yourself and goods.

If your freezer is packed with good food, and your power goes out for a week, you will either need a means of power generation (generator, solar, etc.), or knowledge on how to preserve that food via fermentation, dehydration, salting, or canning.

- Plant a diversity of edible landscaping that produces a variety of crops, even if a storm happens to take some of them out.

- Have candles and lighters stashed in an easy to access area

Know your family and community plan for each disaster scenario such as storm, fire, flood, earthquake, invasion, and pandemic. Challenge: Don't use your phone/computer, a car, or electricity for just one day. Now imagine this for a week or a month. This is what we want to prepare for. Referring to previous chapters, it helps if you **Know your Farmer**, **Plant Seeds**, and **Value Your Neighbor**.

ACTION IDEAS

What is your disacter plan for the above mentioned scenarios? Where will you meet your family and loved ones if we loose communication capabilities? How else will you prepare?

Prepare for Emergencies

53 Be Safe

Recently I shot myself through the thumb with a 2.5″ 16-gauge finish nail while working on a house. I was talking with an old friend I hadn't seen in a while who came to help me finish the job. Our nail gun broke, and while I was fixing it and catching up with him, I shot myself. This is a total rookie mistake, so here is what I should have done.

1. ALWAYS unplug the tool or device when working on it.
2. Stay focused on the task at hand.
3. Keep the pointy side and shooty side facing away from yourself and others.

An old adage holds that *a good woodsman has no less and no more than one bad scar*. An injury, provided we survive it, can awaken us to the power and danger that we work with from day to day. If you've been fortunate enough to make it through life so far without getting your one bad scar, then here, borrow mine.

There are really two kinds of safety: the short term (like I should have used with that nail gun) and the long term. The short term requires focus on the task. The long term requires discipline. Sometimes it's easy to overlook the long-term safety. This is the kind of safety that prevents spinal injury, joint degradation, and all of the other adverse health effects associated with regular use of the body. Some crucial components of long term safety are things like:

1. Stretch before lifting
2. Learn how to lift properly
3. Rest when you need it
4. Stay hydrated
5. Eat healthy food
6. Maintain good posture
7. Physical Therapy - chiropractor, massage etc.

ACTION IDEAS

What is one practice you can commit to doing daily in order to increase both short- and long-term safety?

Be Safe

54 Inspired Learning Daily

After high school, I followed the societal pressures to go to college. When I graduated college, I remember telling myself I was finally done learning. I was so tired of it because I did not enjoy what I was learning. I spent the next couple years of my life pretty stagnant. If I had to do it over again, I would spend a few years traveling around, following my intuition and learning a variety of new skills, languages, cultures, and whatever else my heart desired before I were to embark on a college education.

Learning is so easy now with the internet; it's easy to find podcasts, appropriate Audible books, and useful YouTube content, or to search for subjects directly applicable to what you're experiencing in life. Just check the sources because there is a lot of misinformation.

The key is learning what inspires you. For me, that may vary daily. I have multiple books by my bedside table covering different topics. This chapter is not about making major moves, but tiny micro movements to keep the momentum. One day, I learned the concept of speed reading, which I am still working on increasing, but that one skill has helped me learn more with less time invested. Knowledge truly is a form of wealth.

Challenge: learn something new every day and write it down in a journal.

ACTION IDEAS

What subject inspires you most? What is one step you can take to increase your knowledge and understanding of that subject?

Inspired Learning Daily

55 Leverage Resources

"Given the right lever you can move a planet." ~*Frank Herbert, Author*

Just as a lever or a pulley will increase the amount of weight you can move, you can also leverage your assets, as well as skills and relationships that you already have.

Here are a few ways we leverage our assets that you may want to try.

- Rent out unused rooms to folks looking for short or long-term housing. Some of those are paying guests through AirBnB, and others are people wanting to learn construction and permaculture skills. The skill seekers sometimes work trade for their stay, their food, and classes in topics of interest.

- Our tools are for us to use AND in a tool library for members to rent at a discount. Every person has a daily responsibility to keep the space clean and organized.

- We have a lot of people who say they want to volunteer. Engaging those people for projects is another way we leverage resources. In the past, I have put all of those people in a text group, or a mailing list. It ends up being a win-win situation. We get help on a project. They get a new experience, education and they usually get fed.

We have only begun leveraging, and it is a great way to reduce overall resource necessity while adding value to the community.

ACTION IDEAS

In what ways can you leverage the resources that you already have?

Leverage Resources

56 Build Healthy Soil

If we want to grow and harvest crops, we have to build soil and fertility with time, not destroy it. The only way to reach these endpoints is to improve the life in the soil."
~Elaine Ingham, Microbiologist

Soil is the most important aspect of sustainability. Unhealthy soil is at the root (pun intended) of many of the world's pressing issues. Consider this acronym for SOIL: Sustainable Organic Integrated Livelihoods!

Healthy diverse soil produces healthy diverse food, medicines, and building materials. Soil stores and slowly releases rain water like a sponge. It also acts as a filter with all of the microbial activity it houses, transforming dirty water into clean water. Some of that water then evaporates over time to create moisture in the air, which contributes to cloud cover, then returns to the soil as rain, and the cycle repeats forever. Soil is, in essence, the root of resource production.

The following are a few common **practices that reduce and diminish** soil quality:

- Raking leaves and hauling them off (instead use them as mulch)
- Over-tilling
- Leaving Soil Exposed without ground cover
- Soil compaction with equipment
- Spraying pesticides, fungicides, and herbicides

Now here are a few principles and **methods for building soil**. Keep the ground covered, either through a series of cover crops or mulch. Exposed soil is like an exposed wound. It will deteriorate if not "bandaged" soon. Ammend the soil with things like compost and compost tea, manures minerals, and other mixtures of microorganisms. You could do this manually and or with managed livestock. Add other organic matter too, like mulch, leaves, grass clippings, etc. If you have hard, compacted soils, consider tilling once to loosen it, but beware of the soil loss or compaction that can occur due to tilling when the conditions are not right. You can also loosen soil with a broad fork, or by planting daikon radish or other hardpan penetrating plants.

Check out a documentary called *Back to Eden* with Paul Gautschi, where he shows his development of his fruit orchard by covering the hard packed soil with free mulch from the city.

ACTION IDEAS

What can you do to start building soil in your hometown?

Build Healthy Soil

57 The Energy Matrix

We all spend time doing activities that drain us or consume our energy. And we all have those moment of recharge that get us hyped up and feeling great. For this solution, we will put all of our activities into one giant matrix. The challenge is to energise the matrix with the highest positive number.

First, make a list of all of the things that you do. Next, put a number beside that list between the range of negative five to positive five. The numbers represent how the activity affects you. Negative five is the worst experience and positive five is the best. The idea is for the sum of all activities to be high positive number. This will create a visual for where your energy is flowing to or from and how you can improve upon it.

A simplified example:

Activity	negative	neutral	positive
gardening			3
grocery shopping	-2		
talking with buddy A	-2		
talking with buddy B			5
working out		-1	
being physically fit			5

In the example, grocery shopping is a negative, while gardening is a positve. This person could do less shopping if they did more gardening, thus increasing their matrix. Consider some of the benefits of certain activities as the activity itself such as "being physically fit" as and activity related to "working out". While one action may be a negative, the benefit of that activity may outweigh it in the positive, therefore the negative activity is worth the investment.

In the example of talking with buddy A vs B; without burning a bridge, sometimes it's necessary to take a break from one person and surround yourself with those who help you recharge.

Consider adding some activities that you used to enjoy and may need to rekindle.

ACTION IDEAS

Make your energy matrix below.

The Energy Matrix

58 Embrace Change

"Never doubt that a small group of thoughtful, committed, citizens can change the world. Indeed, it is the only thing that ever has." ~Margaret Mead

The Chinese Taoists and the Greek followers of Heraclitus both arrived at the same conclusion: *Change is the only constant in life.* What that means is that, yes, you *do* have the power to change the world. People do it every day.

There are so many amazing organizations that began as a response to the rapid changing economy of 2008. Once again in 2012, companies were forced to change the way they did business due to the global pandemic. For many the key to survival was embracing the change.

The systems that surround and connect us, including food, communication, transportation, entertainment, and social interactions, are changing constantly. How do we use and respond to that change? We have to open our minds to the possibilities that change can bring. This isn't easy, because change is often uncomfortable, it takes great energy and patience to adjust. It's a little easier to adjust if you can focus on the *functional* qualities of the new change. When faced with something unexpected, even if it seems negative, ask yourself: how can I use this challenge to improve the situation as a whole? What opportunity does this change create and what can we adjust? Make those adjustments, and know that you will have to continue to make them as time moves on.

Consider Climate Change: In the worst projections, many plant and animal species may not survive. This change is very upsetting, but within the parameters of that change, we can focus our efforts on cultivating new species of plants through selective breeding and experimental planting. For instance, water-loving species will die out in a drying environment, but cacti and other drought-tolerant species will thrive. Some cacti are edible, beautiful, and produce fruit and flowers. They are just a little bit different than what you may be used to. Keep planting from seed, as those species can adapt better than cuttings (see **Plant Seeds**). Does this mean we should stop resisting climate change? Of course not. Even in the best projections, the climate will change regardless.

ACTION IDEAS

What are some changes in your life that you may be resisting?

Embrace Change

59 Observe, Then Interact

"Everything that happens, happens as it should, and if you observe carefully, you will find this to be so." ~Marcus Aurelius

The order of this step is crucial: Observe, *then* Interact. Humans tend to interact before they observe.

This entire universe, including you and me, has evolved over billions of years. Everything you see in the natural world has its place in the natural order. This order relies on all elements for it to work efficiently. When you mess up any one element, you mess with the entire system.

This law can be applied not only to interacting with the environment, but with any system: political, social, physical, etc. Suppose, for example, you are hired to be the new director of an established institution. You might be tempted to implement your knowledge and experience immediately and make major changes, because you know your way has worked for you before in a different context. But suppose, as is often the case, that the new institution practices a different work ethic, operates on different hours, or has a very different operating structure than anything you've known. Sure, your experience might offer just the shake-up this institution needs to grow, but if you try to simply dominate the institution, even in small ways at first, you may compromise its integrity and disturb its delicate social and professional ecosystem.

Developing Land: Before you buy and build on a new piece of land, observe it and its surroundings. Sit on the land for weeks, months, or even a year prior to making a move if you can. Ideally, you would observe through all seasons. Observe the wildlife that passes through and what they eat. Observe the sunlight as days pass to locate optimal passive solar areas or garden spots. See how the wind blows in the summer and in the winter. Meet the neighbors and local businesses. Watch it rain and find out where the water goes. Once you have spent adequate time observing, then plan for how you can interact to be the least invasive while improving the quality of the land, in whatever form that may be.

Never stop observing because living systems are in a constant state of flow.

ACTION IDEAS

As you go about your day interacting with people and the environment, what are some observations you've made?

Observe, Then Interact

60 You're In for a Yield

It's easy to get caught up in the routine of doing chores that don't necessarily pay off in the end. The goal is to always produce a yield. Think of a yield as something in excess of what is required to sustain. It's like the profit of the system. It is easier to keep track for short-term projects than it is for long term.

Make a garden diary. Keep record of your time spent doing certain tasks in addition to the resources earned because of that task. For an accurate assessment, do this activity over the time period in which it takes to mature. This, of course can be applied beyond the garden. Some activities are harder to track than others. Here are two easy gardening examples.

Crops: Inputs to consider may be the time, fuel, tractor, soil amendments, seeds, and irrigation. Yields would be the crop itself, and the byproduct. At the end of the period, study the record you made and see if the yields outweigh the inputs. Some other things to consider are the soil quality pre crop vs. post crop, environmental benefits vs. degradation, and the personal enjoyment factor. This is where you can get really subjective if you want.

Egg Production - Inputs to consider might be fencing, coops, guardian animals, food, water, and the cost of the birds. Outputs would be eggs, fertilizer, pest control, and possibly meat. The chickens will not produce eggs for about 5 months, but they produce fertilizer and potential pest control the entire time.

Take a good look at your activities where the input appears to be greater than the output. Can you make adjustments so that they produce a better outcome? Sometimes it's better to find your niche and stick with that, or as I often do, grow the okra and buy the squash.

P.S. You can also **Urine for a Yield**! If you mix 1 part urine with 10 parts water, it makes a great fertilizer. Of course, you would want to use drip irrigation or pour this at the base of the plant.

ACTION IDEAS

What are some activities you do in your daily life where the inputs might outweigh the outputs? What are some adjustments you can make so that your efforts produce a worthwhile yield?

You're In for a Yield

61 Accept Feedback

"We cannot become what we need by remaining what we are." ~*John C Maxwell*

Feedback is key to progress. A very simple feedback loop that we all use at every moment of our lives is the central nervous system. Some feedback we are conscious of, some we are not. We know the brain works with the heart to pump blood, yet we are not constantly conscious of it. However, when we touch a hot iron, we are. Feedback can occur in many ways, but it's always a form of observation. Sometimes the feedback is easy to see, but some feedback may take weeks, months, or even years to see.

Accepting feedback doesn't mean you have to take action on it. Just be open to it. Accepting feedback, in our hot iron example, would be saying "yep, that's hot," while taking action on feedback would be to stop touching the iron. Not all feedback is something you want or need to take action on, and most feedback is not as simple as the hot iron example. You could receive negative feedback like getting stopped for a DUI. While it's easy to run from the negative feedback, consider before discarding that it may provide a foundation for improvement. As a leader in construction and internship programs, I get all kinds of feedback that I do not take action on. Yet the feedback that I am most resistant to is often the most helpful for growth.

If you find yourself in a leadership role, be prepared for lots of feedback. Try to give positive feedback in public and criticism in private. If you are a follower, try to do the same as above, and give the person who you are following an open ear. Listen to what others tell you, or suggest. Ask for others' open input, and try not to get mad at what they say. Pay attention to the books, thoughts, or issues that keep coming up in your life. This step requires you to be open and vulnerable. It allows for major growth for yourself and those around you but it also may be a little uncomfortable at first.

Feedback is not just for failure. Accept feedback for what is successful and build on that. I have a sign on my computer that says "Apply Pareto's principle ALWAYS" Pareto's principle is based on feedback. It's all about eliminating the things that are not serving, and increasing the things that are.

Also, feedback is not just for personal growth. It can be applied to a garden, your family, clients, business, etc.

Try - fail - feedback - improve
Try - succeed - feedback - improve

ACTION IDEAS

What is some feedback you've received lately that is challenging to hear but potentially useful in helping you grow?

Accept Feedback

62 Integrate Appropriately

Initially after taking a permaculture design certification, I was in the mindset to integrate everything. Then after living in the community for 10 years, I realized that separation can be nice, too. Ultimately, I strive for a balance between integration and separation.

I am finding that a degree of separation leads to harmony with instances where people are just too different. For instance, it may be appropriate to separate living spaces of the unorganized from the organized, the frail elderly and the rambunctious kiddos, and the loud late nighters from the early morning risers. Nonetheless, it may be healthy to integrate for social events, work, play, etc. but long periods of integration can lead to insanity, violence and collapse.

Integration, when done well, can take our society to the next level. It requires teamwork and collective thinking. It can create stability and resilience in our agricultural systems and reduce workflow between businesses.

I often hear people say, "when are they going to do something about this?" or "shame on them!" We as individuals need to realize that we are part of them, and every action that we take affects the whole.

Looking to the garden for a solution, we can integrate plants of different kinds into the same garden. Integrate mushrooms, root crops, ground covers, mulches, vines, bushes, understory, overstory plants, mammals, birds, fish, and insects all in one garden. Each element feeds another, and many elements require different resources for survival. Some species will compete with others, so integrating appropriately is key. Now apply the concepts of the garden to people. Integrate people of different cultures to work together, socialize together, and lead together, and our culture can become one of harmony and solution based thinking at every level.

ACTION IDEAS

What are some areas in your life that could be improved by greater integration? Or appropriate segregation?

Integrate Appropriately

63 Problems to Projects

"When something is bad, turn it around and find something good." ~*Daniel Tiger*

In most cases, whatever is causing a problem is integral to the solution. Our first tendency is often to isolate the cause and eliminate it. Instead, let us take a step back and look at the whole picture. Sometimes, we can combine multiple problems and come up with one holistic solution. The projects created out of the solutions will end up being jobs, contributing to a healthy economy.

Let's look at the hot topic of climate change. Some of the problems associated with climate change are rising sea levels, flash flooding, surplus greenhouse gasses, displaced communities, job loss, extreme temperatures, and mass extinction.

One solution that can help with all of that is to **grow more plants.** Growing plants builds soil. Plants and soil absorb greenhouse gasses and store water at higher elevation resulting in less water at sea level. Growing plants on buildings will do the above in addition to regulating building temperature and feeding life. Growing food at home will do yet all of that plus conserve transportation costs for both you and the groceries. We can also grow building materials for displaced communities. There are many abandoned industrial parks that could be re-designed and given to those who are displaced by climate change, not only providing land, but also turning hard surface runoff into luscious landscapes.

Here is a smaller example from my own life:

After the economy crashed in 2008 I was unable to pay my bills. My mortgage was the greatest expense and because housing prices fell 30%, selling the house was not wise. Instead, I began renting rooms. I was able to create enough income to cover the cost of the debt and then some. My new problem became finding the right people to live with. This problem created an opportunity to form an intentional community which immediately led to meeting awesome people. Now 10 years later, I feel so much more fulfilled with our way of life than I ever did before. And the blessings of it all stemmed from one big problem: being unable to pay my bills.

What are some of your biggest problems in life?
What is the worst thing that could happen as a result of the problem?
What is inherent to the problem that can be part of the solution?
What are 3 possible solutions?

ACTION IDEAS

Use the space below to jot down answers to the questions on the previous page.

Problems to Projects

64 Dominion as Stewardship

The idea of humans having dominion over the planet and all living things is nothing new. It's hard to argue with the idea. We are, after all, the species with the most capability of altering our environment. What we can disagree on is what it means to have dominion.

Some people think of dominion as the total supreme hierarchy. I have heard many say that we can destroy the planet and the environment because God will return to fix it all. Imagine God, coming home after a long day's work, only to open the door and find the world that was built to perfection, ground to a pulp.

I like to think of dominion instead as stewardship. As defined by Wikipedia "Stewardship is an *ethic* that embodies the responsible planning and management of resources." Stewardship means we have ability and humility. In a family setting, we have dominion over our children. If we destroy their environment, they will not flourish, but if we are good stewards to their environment, there is no limit to their potential success.

Think of the world like your house. You have dominion over your home just as humans as a species do over the world. We want to take care of our home with regular maintenance, cleaning and care so that it will continue to provide shelter for our family.

If you are stuck in the mindset of having dominion over our planet, I challenge you instead to be a steward of the Earth.

ACTION IDEAS

What are some ways that you can demonstrate good stewardship of the resources you've been entrusted with?

Dominion as Stewardship

65 Expose Bottlenecks

"In most organizations, the bottleneck is at the top of the bottle."
~Peter F. Drucker, Management Consultant and Author

A bottleneck is a restricting point that slows down the flow of progress. To some degree, bottlenecks present as a pattern that arises naturally in many kinds of systems. The work of exposing them, removing them when they are undesirable or harnessing them when they are useful, is a continuous practice and one that requires you to think holistically about a project or problem. Bottlenecks can be tricky and can cascade, or move from one place to another.

Here's an example from personal experience. We were building a house in Ravenel, SC. Three of us were nailing: two with hammers, one with the one nail gun we had. We found it took about ten times as long to drive a nail by hand as it did with the gun. Where's the bottleneck? The first bottleneck is the two workers without a nail gun. A potential solution to this bottleneck would be to get one or two more nail guns. But here it's important to analyze the flow of energy in the system in order to ensure the dependability of this move. Can the air compressor that powers the nail gun(s) keep up? If another nail gun (or two) were purchased without making sure the air compressor could handle the extra load, the air compressor could be the next bottleneck. Other bottlenecks could be the supply of nails or the air hoses.

Bottlenecks are all around us. It may be a point of workflow in your kitchen. Or the number of steps it takes you to get from point A to point B that you end up having to take multiple times daily. It could also be your ability to communicate effectively or a lack of proper supplies to complete a task.

ACTION IDEAS

Throughout the day, try to take note of some bottlenecks that are slowing you down. What can you do to remove the bottleneck and improve efficiency?

Expose Bottlenecks

66 Delegate & Reward

For maximum results, delegate to people that are effective in what they do.

I grew up with the idea that, "If you want something done right, you gotta do it yourself." Now I realize how limiting that idea is to achieving phenomenal results. If a task is simple, it's easy to think, "just do it." But the simple tasks add up, leaving very little time for new experiences. Instead, identify what can be delegated and to whom. It's important to delegate to the right people, otherwise you may end up having to fix a lot of mistakes. Delegating frees up time to focus efforts on the items that need you, and only you. Every task has an associated cost called an opportunity cost, defined as "the loss of potential gain from other alternatives when one alternative is chosen." The opportunity cost of writing this book may be sleeping, exercising, or building something. I cannot delegate sleeping or exercising to someone else, but I can delegate building. A difficult but key ingredient to delegating successfully is to let go of control, at least to a degree.

Make a list of all things that need to be done and label each task based on who you think can help. Learn what inspires your workforce, whether it's your 5 year old who wants to go fishing, an employee who wants a raise, or a friend who wants to learn something new. The best combination for delegating is when someone is proficient at the job while fulfilling their self-worth and keeping the vision on track. Don't forget the reward. For some, the reward is payment. For some, it's going fishing, and for some, it may just be showing appreciation or the experience itself.

Delegation is like a giant puzzle of needs, wants, self-worth, and action.

ACTION IDEAS

What are some tasks that you often do yourself but could instead delegate to another trustworthy person?

Delegate & Reward

67 Facilitate Regeneration

"Surely we have a responsibility to leave for future generations a planet that is healthy and habitable by all species" - Sir David Attenborough

Every ecosystem on our planet has been touched either directly or indirectly by human industry. As a result, many of those systems are in dire need of regeneration. Regeneration is a biological process to restore ecosystems, building resilience to damage and disturbance. The health of each system is key to the balance of the whole.

Think of Earth as a living organism. The land is the skin and the water is the blood. A small cut or scrape will heal, possibly without a scar. Larger cuts require stitches and surgery. If a wound is left untreated, it is likely to get infected. Fracking is like drilling through bone and setting off tiny explosions. Drilling for oil is like harvesting bone marrow. Polluting rivers is like injecting toxins directly into the veins; ocean trash is a chronic blood disease, and a forest fire is like a third degree burn.

Every healthy living thing is capable of regeneration. Earth is ALIVE. Just as one person cannot force another to exercise and eat a nutritionally balanced diet, we cannot FORCE the Earth's systems to be healthy. We can only provide the right environment for it to heal.

The following are some suggestions for regenerative stewardship practices:

- When something is growing, let it grow and observe. What do you notice? What kinds of wildlife are interacting? Does it seem invasive? What does it smell like? Does it produce a fruit, nut, or flower?

- Seed bare soils with nitrogen fixers, wildflowers, and grasses with a focus on native beneficial non-invasive species. If you cannot cover crop, mulch is often a good alternative.

- Explore rapid reforestation strategies with a focus on food forestry and wildlife beneficiary.

- Ditch stream, and river restoration; stop mowing the ditches and create riparian buffer zones around all streams and rivers to filter agricultural and industrial runoff.

Perform micro-surgeries to the landscape to practice the 5 S's of water and increase agricultural production.

Check out some of these real world examples, and for a longer list, go to 71solutions.org

Geoff Lawton's "greening the desert" project in Jordan

Allan Savory and the Savory Institute - reversing desertification

Joel Salatin and Polyface Farm - regenerative agriculture example

Shubhendu Sharma & Afforest - rapid reforestation methodology

Practice regenerations, and Earth can once again be pleasant to the sight and good for food.

ACTION IDEAS

Where might you facilitate regeneration?

Facilitate Regeneration

68 Eat the Weeds

"What is a weed? A plant whose virtues have yet to be discovered."
~Ralph Waldo Emerson

Why we call some green things *plants* and other green things *weeds* has nothing to do with the green things themselves and everything to do with our perception. In this, as in every case, it is a good idea to challenge our perceptions from time to time. The concept of *weed* is a perfect example! Some of the most common *weeds* are actually useful in the sense that they are edible, medicinal, and/or environmentally beneficial plants.

Take the common dandelion, for example. As an herb, dandelion can be used to reduce inflammation. You can dry its roots and grind them to make a coffee-like drink. You can also eat the greens and flowers. This humble, sunny wishing-weed also has physical properties that help build soil and break up compact surfaces. And this very useful plant often grows freely and abundantly in front lawns, often far better than the more showy but almost useless lawn grass. Yet instead of seeing a garden in a field adorned by these yellow blossoms, we have been trained to see a problem. Herbicide containers, accordingly, usually list dandelions as one of the weeds it can kill. Why not *harvest* your front yard instead of poisoning it? Some other common edible weeds growing near us are shiso, lambsquarters, chickweed, maypop, wild lettuce, and greenbrier. Not all weeds are edible, so be sure to identify them properly before consuming.

*Some plants are poisonous and can kill you. Please be sure to positively ID plants before you consume

*Also consider nearby pollutants.

ACTION IDEAS

What are some plants growing in your garden that you tend to perceive as weeds? How might you repurpose them for something beneficial?

Eat the Weeds

69 Recreate Recreation

"People who cannot find time for recreation are obliged to sooner or later find time for illness." ~John Wannamaker, American Pioneer in Marketing

Consider eco friendly alternatives to gas guzzling recreation vehicles. Sailing is one of my favorites. It is quiet, and while sometimes relaxing, it can also be exhilarating. I used to have a pontoon boat that I would take out for fishing trips and pirate parties. Occasionally it would break down and I would have to swim it home. Under normal operation, I had to pour money into the gas tank, just to move it. And eventually, I realized how much pollution it created.

My idea of recreation changed when a friend took me sailing for my birthday. I LOVED it, but I didn't really learn to sail until I got a small boat of my own. Day 1 of my solo sailing adventure, I broke my pinky toe when the boat nearly capsized. Day 2, I was blown out to an island. Day 2.5, I learned how to sail so I could get back home. If you choose to sail, you may consider spending more time with the person who knows how to sail before taking your own solo adventure.

Sailing offers great connection to the spirit of nature. Conversations can unfold, music can be enjoyed, and food can be cooked underway, all while observing the wildlife around you. The joy is in the journey.

I love the practicality of sailboats. It's like a tiny house on water. There is something special about sleeping on the water, feeling the wind blow and the flow of the water, then waking up to the sunlight beaming through the fog with wildlife close by, undisturbed by the silence of our presence.

Think about investigating forms of recreation that are Earth-friendly. Some other suggestions might be canoeing, kayaking, paddle boarding, windsurfing, kiteboarding, biking and hiking. Whatever you do, tread lightly, and please leave nature better than you found it.

ACTION IDEAS

What is one form of earth-friendly recreation that you can try out today?

70 Stick to the List

"Find a list method that works for you. Doodles, Bullet-points, charts, what suits you best?" - Sir Richard Branson, British Business Magnate

Have you ever gone shopping and ended up with more than what you need? Or woke up with an intention to do something, but end up completely distracted?

Before making a list, It can be helpful to identify your goals. Once complete, the only things that go on the list are to help you accomplish your goal.

Here are a few apps that I find helpful, especially when integrated with each other.

Toodledo to organize the task lists based on goals and contexts while assigning due dates and priorities.

Evernote for things like groceries or materials, books to read, movies, places to visit, etc.

Calendar for long term planning, birthdays, meetings, classes, and events.

What are your top goals? What is on your list? Does the item, errand, or purchase help you accomplish your goals? If no, then don't go there, buy it, or do that. This will help you stay focused, fulfilled, and efficient. With groceries, what do you want to eat that you know is healthy? Put that on the list, and stick to it. Make a list for what you want to accomplish today and do that.

ACTION IDEAS

Use this space to answer the questions on the previous page.

Stick to the List

71 Unite

United we stand, divided we fall

We all have so much in common, yet we tend to focus on what divides us. The media in general doesn't help, but the media is not entirely to blame. It is natural to focus on the bad. Unless we step on a thorn, we hardly notice our feet. The same goes for society. If there is trouble, the whole world knows, but good news will not travel far.

Power in unity is an idea that has been traced back as early as Aesop's fables, written between 620 and 564 BCE. A phrase like "United we stand, divided we fall" has been used in numerous literary works and motivational speeches throughout history. In the United States we know this phrase from one of our founding fathers, John Dickinson. The reason it is so widely used, I believe, is because it's a natural principle. Permaculture refers to it as the edge effect. If we break something up into smaller pieces, it will be easy to infiltrate, decompose, or incinerate. Take a block of wood. As a whole, it's difficult to catch fire. Broken up into pieces, it will burn quickly.

Steer clear of the media that is intended to divide us. We will certainly crumble as a society if we focus on our disagreements. If any person or periodical is downplaying someone or something else, disregard it because there is likely an agenda. Instead, search for the non-biased scientific research.

I would like to end by urging you to collaborate with people whom you would generally disagree with and focus instead on what you have in common. If we focus on unity, we can accomplish anything.

"Alone we can do so little; together we can do so much." ~Helen Keller

ACTION IDEAS

Now that you've read through *71 Solutions*, what will your next step be to integrate and implement what you've learned?

Unite

Afterword

I hope this book has provided value in a way that helps you live in peace, prosperity, and harmony with our planet. Please share the book and engage with us on the forum at 71Solutions.org to tell your stories, challenges, and successes through your journey. As Joseph McClendon III would say, "Life is exactly what you dare to make it, and fortune favors the bold." So boldly take action to be a positive impact for yourself, our home, and your fellow humans.

Glossary

Absolute abundance: where there lies plenty of everything necessary for survival

Amity: peaceful and harmonious relationships, especially between nations

Benefit Corporations: mission-driven businesses and certified through a process of in depth analysis focused on doing business that is good for people and the planet. Buy the change you want to see in the world!

Ecosystems: a biological community of interacting organisms and their physical environment

Internatural: between, among, and mutually with nature

Permaculture: a whole system nature mimicry design science used to improve efficiency, beauty, and functionality

Resilience: the capacity to recover quickly from difficult situations

Self-sufficient: to provide everything you need for yourself

Sustainable: to respect and live in harmony with our planet and all other living things